$8.95

The canoes of John Henry Rushton of Canton, New York, have been admired and coveted since they were first built more than a hundred years ago. Their smooth lapstrake cedar planking, fine craftsmanship, and light weight appealed to canoeing enthusiasts across the country. Rushton's catalogs of his wares described and demonstrated the traditional techniques of his boatshop—and the 1903 catalog, reproduced here, includes a typical selection of Rushton craft. William Crowley, the Curator of The Adirondack Museum, Blue Mountain Lake, New York, has provided a scene-setting Introduction to Rushton and his era, illustrated by 12 photographs from the Museum's collection.

Rushton's pride in the quality of his craft was best summed up on the first page of this 1903 catalog: "No other establishment in the world can give you the same service that I can."

INTERNATIONAL MARINE PUBLISHING COMPANY
Camden, Maine

ISBN 0-87742-164-1

RUSHTON'S

Rowboats and Canoes

J. Henry Rushton, ca. 1903

RUSHTON'S

ROWBOATS AND CANOES

THE 1903 CATALOG IN PERSPECTIVE

WILLIAM CROWLEY

THE ADIRONDACK MUSEUM
Blue Mountain Lake, New York

INTERNATIONAL MARINE PUBLISHING COMPANY
Camden, Maine

Published by International Marine Publishing Company
21 Elm Street, Camden, Maine 04843
(207) 236-4342

John Henry Rushton
Adirondack Boatbuilder

by William Crowley
Curator, The Adirondack Museum

John Henry Rushton (1843–1906) became one of the country's preeminent boatbuilders almost by accident. The son of a cabinetmaker in the northern New York village of Canton, he spent his childhood hunting and fishing on the numerous lakes and streams of the northern Adirondacks. He and his friends had built their own dugout or spruce bark canoes to take on their expeditions.

But the Adirondack topography, dotted with 2,300 lakes and ponds and few roads, presented problems to the sportsman and explorer. The easiest means of travel through the region was by water, but this involved a number of portages or "carries" between the lakes and rivers. A portable boat, light yet durable, was essential.

This need led to the development of the Adirondack guideboat, which achieved lightness through the use of thin planking, set lapstrake but smooth, and slender ribs sawn from the roots of spruce stumps. In his late twenties, Rushton began building boats for himself; he developed his own lightweight variation of traditional lapstrake construction. The key to his method was the use of small, steam-bent, half-round ribs. Strength was achieved by spacing the ribs only 1½ to 3 inches apart. He used northern white cedar for planking because he felt it gave the most strength for the least weight.

The result was a lightweight but somewhat unsteady boat. As he described one of his early craft:

'It was light; but part your hair in the middle, and you fellow in the bow, mind that you shoot straight ahead, else over you go.'' After several more attempts, Rushton produced a boat that satisfied him. Perhaps with some exaggeration, he claimed to have developed a boat that was steady in the water, weighed only 39 pounds, and was capable of carrying four (!) men.

A friend saw the boat and demanded that he be allowed to buy it. Rushton built a second one for himself but soon found customers eager for all that he could build. Thus, willy-nilly, Rushton became a commercial boatbuilder. The style of these early craft is unknown. They may have been rowboats, canoes, or some combination thereof.

It seems likely that Rushton sold that first boat about 1873; for the next few years he sold his craft only to local buyers. In 1876, A.H. Siegfried of Louisville, Kentucky, asked Rushton to build a lighter-weight version of one of two well-known English cruising canoes, John MacGregor's *Rob Roy* and Warrington Baden-Powell's *Nautilus*. In what may have been his first attempt at building canoes, Rushton supplied two hulls, 13 feet long by 30 inches wide, which weighed only 35 pounds each. Siegfried and his friend J.H. Barnes decked the hulls with canvas, fitted them with masts, and then sailed and paddled them from Hornell, New York, to the Philadelphia Exposition.

It is interesting to note the English origin of these craft and, indeed, of canoeing as a sport. Contrary to popular belief, the early recreational canoes were not modeled after the native American birchbark canoe. Combination sailing and paddling canoes, first developed in England in the 1860s, were popularized by MacGregor and Baden-Powell, who used their craft to explore the inland and coastal waterways of Europe. In 1866, MacGregor published a small book chronicling his experiences entitled *A Thousand Miles in the Rob Roy Canoe on Twenty Rivers and Lakes of Europe*. Subsequently serialized in *Harper's* magazine, the narrative did much to popularize recreational canoeing in the United States.

Rushton published his first catalog of boats in 1877. He offered double-ended rowboats in six sizes, a 14-foot Rob Roy model sailing canoe, and a 13-foot open canoe. The title of that catalog, *Rushton's Portable Sporting Boats and Canoes*, emphasized the portability of his craft, developed for the Adirondack environment.

In the years following Siegfried's trip to Philadelphia, several other venturesome voyages of exploration brought Rushton's craft to national attention. In 1879, Siegfried, Barnes, and Lucien Wulsin took three Rushton Rob Roys to Lake Itasca, Minnesota, near the source of the Mississippi, and then cruised down that river as far as Aitkin, Minnesota. In 1881, Willard Glazier used another Rob Roy to travel the same river from Aitkin to the Gulf of Mexico. Most ambitious of all was Charles A. Neidé's 3,300-mile voyage in a Rushton Princess model canoe from Lake George in the Adirondacks down the Mississippi and to Pensacola, Florida. All three trips were covered by the national press, and both Glazier and Neidé published books on their adventures.

Most important of all in focusing national attention upon Rushton and establishing his reputation as the preeminent builder of lightweight canoes were the letters of George Washington Sears published in *Forest and Stream* magazine. Sears, who wrote under the pen name of Nessmuk, wanted to explore the waters of the Adirondacks on his own without the help of a guide. Fifty-nine years old, small of stature, and in poor health, Sears felt he needed a canoe weighing less than 20 pounds — something unheard-of at the time. Rushton agreed to give it a try, although he refused to guarantee that the craft would last an hour.

The result, the *Wood Drake*, or Nessmuk No. 1, was 10 feet long, had a 26-inch beam, and weighed just under 18 pounds. She carried the 105-pound Sears and about 40 pounds of gear throughout much of the Adirondacks in the summer of 1880. Surpassing her builder's expectations, the *Wood Drake* "came out tight and staunch" at the end of the cruise. In all, Rushton built five small canoes for Sears, who used them to explore the Adirondacks in 1880, 1881, and 1883 and the coastal waters of Florida in 1885.

Rushton began offering the extremely lightweight Nessmuk canoes in his 1881 catalog. The *Sairy Gamp*, built for Sears in 1883, was 9 feet long and weighed only 10½ pounds. She is now on display at the Adirondack Museum.

Rushton was acquiring a national reputation for building lightweight canoes designed for the explorer of the nation's waterways. The combination sailing and paddling canoe, or "cruiser," as Rushton called it, became his specialty.

Equally important to the success of his business was Rushton's astute grasp of marketing techniques. Advertising was coming into its own in the 1870s, and Rushton regularly advertised his boats in such specialized sporting magazines as *Forest and Stream* and *The Rudder*. He produced his first mail-order catalog at about the same time as Montgomery Ward and Sears started their catalogs. His displays at the Philadelphia and Columbian Expositions also helped to publicize his boats.

Rushton's involvement in the newly formed American Canoe Association also enhanced his reputation. He was one of 23 founding members of the ACA who first met at Lake George in August of 1880. From the start, Rushton craft figured prominently in the many sailing and paddling races at ACA meets held each year at such places as Lake George and the St. Lawrence River. Participation in the Association provided Rushton with free publicity and allowed him to test and compare his work against that of other builders.

Rushton craft achieved their greatest racing successes in the years 1885 and 1886. In 1885, Robert W. Gibson of the Mohican Canoe Club sailed and paddled a Rushton Mohican No. 1 to first place in the overall ACA point standings. The following year, Gibson sailed his Rushton-built *Vesper* to victory in the first of two international challenge cup races, while another Rushton craft won the overall championship. Gibson was beaten, however, by E.H. Barney's *Pecowsic* in a second, unscheduled race at the same meet. Built by Fletcher Joyner of

Glens Falls, New York, the *Pecowsic* was a specialized racing craft unsuitable for general use, while Rushton's all-purpose paddling and sailing canoes were designed primarily for cruising. After 1886, the ACA events were increasingly dominated by specialized sailing canoes designed for racing only and by open paddling canoes constructed along the lines of Canadian models.

In 1893, Rushton attempted to meet this challenge by introducing two sailing canoes specially designed for racing, but his craft were unable to match their earlier records in ACA competition. He was more successful with a line of open Canadian-model canoes, which he began to develop in 1887. Rushton's business continued to prosper. He introduced new product lines, including duckboats; launches powered by steam, electricity, and naphtha; dinghies; catboats; large sailing cruisers; and even a folding boat. In 1886, he also offered toboggans for sale, and in 1895 he attempted to sell packbaskets made by St. Regis Indians.

As the business grew, Rushton found it necessary to expand his facilities and to hire additional craftsmen. He hired his first workman, Nelson Brown, in 1877, and by 1881 had six people in his employ. He built a new workshop in 1881 and had 20 men working for him by 1887. The following description of the shop appeared in the April 6, 1882, issue of *Forest and Stream*:

. . . Rushton carries in stock something like 150 canoes, and sells them like hot cakes every spring, and with a score of hands cannot keep pace with the demand. Labor-saving machinery of all kinds has been introduced and canoes are now set up and finished off wholesale, in fleets at a time, though each one receives that personal care and supervision which has given to Rushton's work such an enviable reputation. His "factory" consists of a main building three stories high, 80 ft. long and 30 ft. wide, with two wings, each 24 ft. long and 18 ft. wide. The cellar is used for seasoning timber by furnace or kiln and other processes. The first story is devoted to the receipt and storage of lumber, dressed and undressed; also for oars, paddles, keels, paints, and for material for boxing. The second story is given up to general work. In one wing is a steam-boiler and fixtures, with machines for ribbing the boats by Rushton's patent method, and also appliances for bending timber to suitable forms. In the other wing are the offices, drawing room, and sleeping apartments. The third story is used for storage and finishing of boats, painting, varnishing, and the like. The attic is the receptacle for patterns. There is about these shops at present a buzz of activity which augurs well for the coming season and for the vast patronage bestowed by the public upon this enterprising builder and successful business man. To Mr. Rushton's personal interest in behalf of canoeing the sport owes no little of its present popularity and the deep root it has taken with the masses of our population.

A turning point occurred in 1893, when Rushton borrowed heavily to publish a greatly expanded catalog and to take an exhibit to the Columbian Exposition in Chicago. The financial panic of that year caused a severe economic depression, which, combined with a burgeoning craze for a new outdoor sport, bicycling, led to a decline in Rushton's business.

It took him several years to recover his losses and repay the loan. By that time, the era of the venturesome explorer who required an all-purpose sailing and paddling canoe seems to have come to an end. Increasingly, the market focused upon the casual canoeist who wanted a cheap, open paddling canoe. For years Rushton had resisted wood-and-canvas construction, insisting that the fine craftsmanship and lighter weight of his all-wood canoes justified the greater expense. He finally succumbed to increasing competition and introduced his own line of wood-and-canvas models about 1902. The Indian and subsequent Indian Girl lines quickly became the most important part of the business. A wood-and-canvas Indian cost little more than half the price of the all-cedar model.

John Henry Rushton died on May 1, 1906. The firm, run by family members, continued in operation until 1916. Rushton began building boats at the very start of sport canoeing in America. His construction techniques and designs contributed greatly to the development of the craft. He has left a legacy of well-designed and finely crafted boats, many of which are still in use on the waters of his native Adirondacks.

RUSHTON'S CATALOG FOR 1903

The 1903 catalog, reproduced from an original in the Adirondack Museum Library, shows a typical selection of Rushton craft. The fact that he offered only two cruising canoes is indicative of how the market had changed over the years. The all-purpose sailing and paddling canoe had given way to the specialized racing craft and the open paddler, especially the cheaper wood-and-canvas models. His reluctance to adopt wood-and-canvas construction is reflected in both his comments about lapstrake construction (*page 5*) and his discussion concerning canvas-covered canoes (*page 43*).

Rushton's introductory remarks in the preface (*pages 3-5*) provide an excellent summary of his philosophy of boatbuilding and his belief in craftsmanship. Although he had reduced the number of models from previous years, Rushton was still will-

ing to make other types of boats on special order. His willingness to experiment was characteristic of Rushton throughout his career. Some of his most successful models, such as the Vesper and the Nessmuk series, sprung from others' ideas, although Rushton always claimed that the final designs were his own.

Rushton made the same claim for much of the boat hardware listed on pages 62-79. In his 1890 catalog, he stated that, "It is a fact worthy of attention that at least three-fourths of all the so called 'canoe jewelry' originated in our factory. Not being protected by patents, the various articles have become public property."

The variety of construction grades offered in the catalog differs mostly in the quality of materials and often reflects a desire for greater beauty rather than any major difference in the strength of the boat. Evidently there were people who admired the beauty of Rushton's workmanship as well as the quality of his construction and the practicality of his designs.

Pleasure Boats

The Rushton pleasure boats are probably the closest in design to the first boats he made, although they are much heavier than his original 35-pound models. Calling them "portable row boats," he offered six sizes in his initial catalog of 1877. Although the number and variety of models changed from year to year, this line of craft remained essentially the same throughout Rushton's lifetime. Beginning in 1883, Rushton built them square-sterned as well as double-ended. From 1887 onward, they could be ordered with smooth or semismooth planking as well as the traditional lapstrake planking. In 1890, he introduced a line of combination row and sail boats based on the hulls of the pleasure boats. In 1895, he began designating the various models by the use of state names. At that point, he was offering 10 models in a variety of sizes, including a St. Lawrence River Skiff. Both the Islander and Livery models were introduced sometime between 1895 and 1903. Rushton introduced a Dinghy about 1890, in both double-ended and square-sterned models. The Cat Boat was developed sometime between 1895 and 1903. It was dropped from the Rushton catalogs in 1908.

Guideboats

Although included under the category of "pleasure row boats," the Adirondack or Saranac Lake Boat deserves special attention. Based on the traditional Adirondack guideboat, this extremely lightweight craft derived its strength from the use of natural-crook ribs or knees rather than the close spacing of steam-bent ribs. When Rushton introduced this craft in 1888, he described it as "... a very light swift boat. A little more cranky than our other models, but faster." Rushton's preference for his own style of construction is reflected in the fact that he gradually reduced the rib spacing of this craft from seven to four inches and eventually offered a model with steam-bent ribs.

Open Canoes

In 1887, Rushton began offering open paddling canoes based on what he called "the Canadian rib and batten canoe." It was not until 1892 that this type of craft (characterized by smooth planking, tumblehome stems, and flat bottoms) became a regular feature in his catalogs. In that same year, he began offering a few models, called "racing paddlers," with finer lines and less weight. The Igo and Ugo, which appeared about 1895, probably derive from these models. The Arkansaw Traveler, an even lighter version, was developed sometime between 1895 and 1903. The Ontario is probably based on Rushton's earlier Canadian models.

The origins of the lightweight or Nessmuk canoes have already been discussed. The Nessmuk model was offered for the first time in 1881 and the Bucktail in 1885. The Vaux was introduced in 1891 and the St. Regis in 1895. The Vaux, Jr. and the Huron were developed sometime between 1895 and 1903.

In the introduction to his catalog for 1887, Rushton states: ". . . to say that any canvas canoe ever built is little, if any, inferior to our fine cedar ones, is to say that a wall tent is as good as a 'brownstone front.' There may be times and places where the tent would even be preferred, but for steady business give us something more substantial than cloth for use on land or water." He continued to hold this belief throughout his lifetime.

Nonetheless, Rushton began developing a canvas-covered canoe about 1900. Based upon the birch-bark canoe, the Indian model was first offered to the public in 1902. He introduced the Indian Girl (available only in canvas) in 1903, and it soon became the mainstay of the boatshop. In 1905, he built a few canvas-covered sailing canoes and rowboats.

As mentioned previously, Rushton had two cruising canoes for sale in 1903. The Vesper, originally designed by R.W. Gibson and built by Rushton, was first offered to the public in 1887. Over the years, six different sizes were sold. The 16-foot model shown in this catalog was developed sometime between 1895 and 1903. The Wren seems to have been an experimental model and was replaced by the Nomad in 1905.

A brief comment ought to be made concerning the prices in the 1903 catalog. Today, a qualified crafts-man would have to charge $3,000 to $4,000 for a boat that Rushton sold in 1903 for under $200. But, of course, the value of the dollar has changed dramatically over the years — $20 a week was con-sidered a good wage for a skilled worker at that time. Rushton, for example, was paying his workers 15 cents an hour in 1893.

Although aluminum and fiberglass canoes now dominate the market, there has been a gratifying resurgence of interest in classic wooden boats. Since Rushton was a premier builder of wooden canoes and rowboats, his craft now are sought eagerly by collectors. The beauty and craftsmanship of his work can be seen in the Adirondack Museum's collection of more than 25 of his boats. They reflect the philosophy of boatbuilding he stated in 1882:

We think we quote from an esteemed contemporary — and a gentlemen [sic] withall — when we say "The keel of the perfect canoe has not yet been laid." We intend to approach perfection as near as possible aided by several years of study, observation of all the principal models both on shore and in friendly contest with each other, the advice and comments by letter and in person of hundreds of prominent canoeists and the assistance of an able corps of skilled and experienced workmen.

Perhaps Rushton did not achieve the perfection he continually sought to attain, but his craft, particularly his canoes, have rarely been surpassed by other wooden boats.

SUGGESTED READINGS

Brenan, Dan. *The Adirondack Letters of George Washington Sears: Whose Pen Name Was Nessmuk.* Blue Mountain Lake, NY: The Adirondack Museum, 1962.

Glazier, Willard. *Down the Great River.* Philadelphia: Hubbard Brothers, 1892.

Manley, Atwood. *Rushton and His Times in American Canoeing.* Syracuse: The Adirondack Museum/ Syracuse University Press, 1968.

Neidé, Charles A. *Canoe Aurora: A Cruise from the Adirondacks to the Gulf.* New York: Forest and Stream, 1885.

Rushton, John Henry. "How I Came to be a Canoe Builder." *The American Canoeist,* February 1882.

RUSHTON ALBUM

Rushton boatshop, Canton, New York: built 1881, closed 1916. J. Henry Rushton stands to the right of the tree in the foreground.

J. Henry Rushton and his workmen, about 1904. Rushton is standing in the front row, extreme left. His son, Harry Rushton, stands behind him.

Charles A. Neidé in the Aurora, a Rushton Princess model that he sailed 3,300 miles from Lake George, New York, to Pensacola, Florida, in 1882-83.

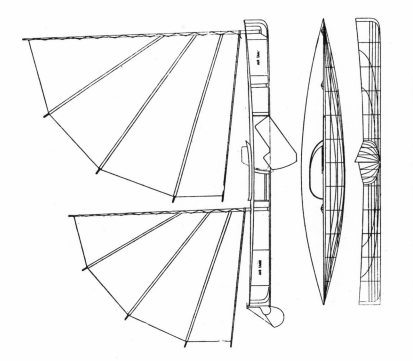

Rushton racing canoe Torpedo, from the 1893 catalog.

39 RIBS 7/16 X 5/32
FASTENED IN PLACE
AFTER PLANKING IS
CLOUT-NAILED. NO INSIDE
GUNWALE STRIP.

3/4 x 1 3/4 KEEL-KEELSON IS
RABBETED TO RECEIVE
GARBOARD STRAKE AND
PROVIDE 3/4W KEEL WHICH
PROJECTS 3/16.

#1 #2 #3 #4 #3 #2 #1

18 12 12 12 12 12 12 18

9'-0"

STEM STARTS

6 7/8

9"x26" RUSHTON CANOE "SAIRY GAMP"
AT THE ADIRONDACK MUSEUM
ON LOAN FROM THE SMITHSONIAN INSTITUTION
OFFSETS AND DRAWINGS BY O.E. MARKKULA
5/19/67

Canoe Sairy Gamp, built by Rushton and used by George Washington Sears
("Nessmuk") in 1883. The canoe is on exhibit at The Adirondack Museum.
(Drawings courtesy) Syracuse University Press)

OFFSETS FOR 7-STATION FORM 9"x26" RUSHTON CANOE "SAIRY GAMP" AT THE ADIRONDACK MUSEUM

ON LOAN FROM THE SMITHSONIAN INSTITUTION

OFFSETS AND DRAWINGS BY O.E.MARKKULA

ELEVATIONS ABOVE BASE	FORM 4 MIDSHIP 1 REQ'D.	FORM 3 12"to4 2 REQ'D.	FORM 2 12"to3 2 REQ'D.	FORM 1 12"to2 2 REQ'D.
	HALF–WIDTHS OUTSIDE SURFACE OF PLANKING			
2	8	6¼	1½	
3	10¼	8⅜	5-	1 7/16
4	11¼	10⅝	7 1/16	2½
5	11⅞	11 5/16	9¼	4 7/16
6	12⅜	11⅞	10⅛	5 13/16
7	12 9/16	12⅛	10⅞	6 7/16
8	12¾	12¼	10⅞	6 9/16
8¾	*13 3/16			
9		*12⅝	11-	7 1/16
9⅞			*10½	
11¼				*7⅜

* AT GUNWALE HEIGHT.

a) PLANKING IS LAPSTRAKE 5/32" THICK WITH 6 STRAKES ON EACH SIDE BECOMING BEVELED-LAP AT STEMS.

OUTSIDE CENTER-LINE ELEVATIONS ABOVE BASE — KEEL AND STEM 9"X26" RUSHTON CANOE "SAIRY GAMP"

MEASUREMENTS AND DRAWINGS BY O.E.MARKKULA

O.S. ℄ — KEEL

STATION NO. OR INCHES FROM NO.1	ELEV. ABOVE BASE
NO.4	1⅜
NO.3	1 7/16
NO.2	1¾
NO.1	2-
NO.1 + 10½ ⊘	2½

⊘ END OF RABBETED KEEL—KEELSON. 1¾ X ¾ X 7'-9". O.S. KEEL ¾ WIDE—EXTENDS 5/16"

O.S. ℄ — STEM

STATION (INCHES FROM STATION 1)	ELEV. ABOVE BASE
NO.1 + 10½	2½
" + 11⅞	3
" + 12¾	4
" + 13⅜	5
" + 14 1/16	6
" + 14 9/16	7
" + 15⅛	8
" + 15⅝	9
" + 18-	14½

NOTE: RABBETED STEM 1⅛" WIDE STARTS AT 1+6⅞

GENERAL NOTE:
STEAMED RIBS 7/16 X 5/32 SPACED 2⅝ ON CENTERS, FASTENED IN PLACE AFTER PLANKING AND AFTER REMOVAL FROM FORM.

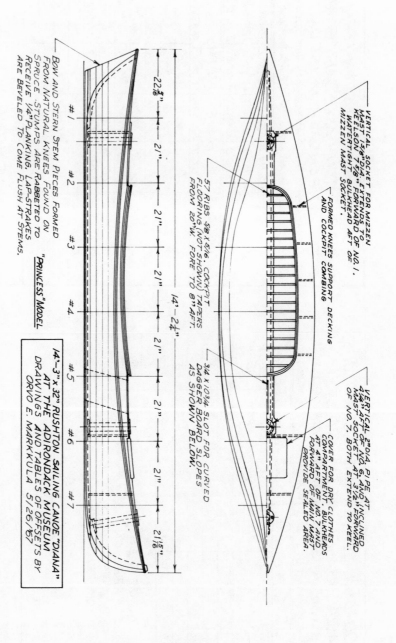

VERTICAL SOCKET FOR MIZZEN
MAST 1⅜" DIA. EXTENDS TO
KEELSON 7⅝" FORWARD OF NO. 1.
WATERTIGHT BULKHEAD AFT OF
MIZZEN MAST SOCKET.

FORMED KNEES SUPPORT DECKINGS
AND COCKPIT COMBING

VERTICAL 2" DIA. PIPE AT
4¼" AFT OF NO. 6, AND INCLINED
MAST SOCKET AT 3½" FORWARD
OF NO. 7, BOTH EXTEND TO KEEL.

COVER FOR DRY CLOTHES
COMPARTMENT. BULKHEADS
AT 4" AFT OF NO. 7 AND
FORWARD OF MAIN MAST
PROVIDE SEALED AREA.

BOW AND STERN STEM PIECES FORMED
FROM NATURAL KNEES FOUND ON
SPRUCE . STUMPS ARE RABBETED TO
RECEIVE ¼" PLANKING. LAP-STRAKES
ARE BEVELED TO COME FLUSH AT STEMS.

57 RIBS ⅝ x ⁵⁄₁₆. COCKPIT
FLOORING (NOT SHOWN) TAPERS
FROM 20" W. FORE TO 8" AFT.

¾ x 10¾ SLOT FOR CURVED
DAGGER BOARD SLOPES
AS SHOWN BELOW.

22⅝"

21"

21"

21"

21"

21"

21"

21⅝"

14'- 24"

"PRINCESS" MODEL

#1 #2 #3 #4 #5 #6 #7

14'-3" x 32" RUSHTON SAILING CANOE "DIANA"
AT THE ADIRONDACK MUSEUM
DRAWINGS AND TABLES OF OFFSETS BY
ORVO E. MARKKULA 5/26/67

Canoe Diana, the first Princess model canoe built for Lucien Wulsin. It is now on exhibit at The
Adirondack Museum. (Drawings courtesy Syracuse University Press)

OFFSETS for 7-STATION FORM 14'-3"x32" RUSHTON CANOE "DIANA" AT THE ADIRONDACK MUSEUM

TABLES OF OFFSETS AND DRAWINGS BY ORVO E.MARKKULA   8/21/'67

HALF-WIDTHS — OUTSIDE SURFACE OF PLANKING — FORMS SPACED 21" TO ¢

ELEV. ABOVE BASE	#1	#2	#3	#4	#5	#6	#7
BASE							
2	1 7/16	5 9/16	11 1/2	13 3/8	11 1/2	5 7/16	1 1/2
4	2 7/8	9 3/8	13 5/8	15 3/16	13 11/16	9 7/16	3 1/4
6	4 1/4	11	14 5/8	15 11/16	14 11/16	11 3/16	4 3/16
8	5 9/16	11 3/4	15 1/8	16	15	12 1/4	6 3/8
10	6 5/16	12 1/8	14 7/8	15 1/2	14 3/4	12 1/2	6 15/16
*11				*16 1/16			
*11 1/4			*15 3/16				
*1 5/8					15 1/8		
12	6 3/4	12 1/2				12 5/16	7 3/8
*13 1/2						*12 7/16	
14							7 5/8
*14 7/8	*7 3/8						
*16 1/2							7 7/8

* OUTSIDE EDGE GUNWALE TOP.
PINE DECKING COVERS ROUNDED GUN'L STRIP WHICH IS 1/2 x 3/4.
b) ALSO GUNWALE WIDTH AT 12 3/4 ELEV.
COCKPIT COMBING 2 1/2 x 3/8 WITH 1/2 x 3/8 REINFORCING AROUND OUTSIDE TOP.

OUTSIDE CENTER-LINE ELEVATIONS ABOVE BASE—KEEL AND STEMS 14'-3"x32" RUSHTON SAILING CANOE "DIANA"

MEASUREMENTS AND DRAWINGS BY O.E.MARKKULA

O.S. ¢ — KEEL		STERN & BOW STEMS			
FORM NO.	ELEV. ABOVE BASE	STERN IN. FROM #1 O.S.¢	RABBET	ELEV. ABOVE BASE	BOW STEM IN. FROM #7 TO O.S. ¢
a)#1-15 3/8	1/2			1 1/4	a)#7+9 5/8
#1	5/16	-16	-5 3/4	2	+13
#2	5/16	-16 3/4	-10	4	+16 1/16
#3	5/16	-17 5/8	-12 3/4	6	+18 1/2
#4	5/16	-18 1/2	-14 9/16	8	+19 5/8
#5	5/16	-19 1/4	-16 3/8	10	+20 1/4
#6	3/8	-20	-17 3/4	12	+20 1/2
#7	3/4	-20 3/8	-18 5/8	14	+21
a)#7+9 5/8	1 1/4	-21 5/8	-20	16	+21 3/8
b)		-22 9/16		18	+21 11/16
				20	+21 7/8
				20 5/8	b) +21 15/16

a) KEEL END
b) END GUNWALE TOP

KEEL WIDTHS AT STATIONS SHOWN (RABBETED KEEL-KEELSON PROJECTS 3/8")

STATION #	1-15 3/8	1	2	3	4	5	6	7	7+9 5/8
KEEL WIDTH	5/8	1 1/4	2	2 1/4	2 5/8	2 1/2	2 1/2	1 1/8	5/8

American Canoe Association (ACA) review, 1885. (Stoddard photo)

Maneuvering under sail, 1885 ACA meet. (Stoddard photo)

Rushton tent at 1886 ACA meet. Rushton is third from right.

ACA members at 1888 meet. Five ACA founders are in photograph, including J. Henry Rushton (front row, seated sideways, second from right).

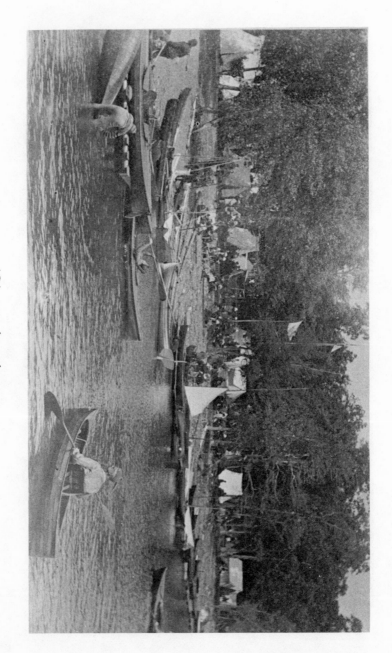

ACA camp, date unknown.

ACA camp, 1887.

Mohican Canoe Club in war canoe, 1891 ACA meet.

Canoe Dimple, 1888 ACA meet. (Stoddard photo)

RUSHTON'S ROWBOATS & CANOES

CATALOGUE
OF HIGH GRADE
ROWBOATS AND CANOES.

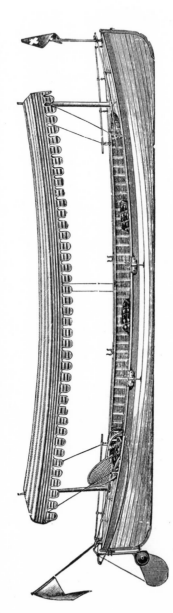

I occupy 16,500 square feet floor space, exclusive of basements, lumber sheds and winter storage for stock boats. No other establishment in the world can give you the same service that I can.

I BUILD NO POWER BOATS OF ANY KIND.

Address,

J. H. RUSHTON,

CANTON, ST. LAWRENCE COUNTY, N. Y.,

TAKE NOTICE.

I HEREBY WITHDRAW AND CANCEL ALL PRICES, DISCOUNTS AND TERMS MADE PRIOR TO 1903.

J. H. RUSHTON.

TERMS OF SALE AND PAYMENT—DISCOUNT.

All sales are made on a strictly NET CASH basis. Orders will be accepted for goods for future delivery on payment of 25 pet cent., balance to be paid at date of delivery. I deliver goods at the office of the New York Central and Hudson River R. R. Co., or American Express Company in Canton. Hence payment is due on shipment. These terms are necessary, as my retail trade is largely with people of whose responsibility I know nothing. Often I do not even know what part of the world they reside in, as their order is written, perhaps, from some summer hotel or woods camp, while their home may be anywhere from Maine to California. In such cases purchasers should give their home address, and if not in trade refer to some Bank, establish proper credit by such reference *unless entirely satisfied* to prepay. Shipments C. O. D. or on Bill of Lading must be protected by payment sufficient to cover transportation both ways.

DISCOUNTS—*Only to dealers.* The lists are net for all retail trade.

PACKING FOR SHIPMENT—The ALL WOOD BOATS AND CANOES are *crated* free of charge to the purchaser and no charge is made for packing masts, sails, oars, &c., &c., if sold separate from boats. BUT a charge is made for crating or packing ALL CANVAS COVERED CANOES, and if all wood boats are packed in Burlap and Excelsior (as for shipment by express) a charge of from one to two dollars, according to size of boat, will be made.

GREETING.

To My Friends and Patrons:

It is many years since I first began to whittle NORTHERN WHITE CEDAR into shape for the various parts of a boat.

It is almost thirty years since this whittling assumed such shape and proportions as to be called *Business.* During that time I have built a very great variety as well as number of small craft. They have gone to all parts of the world and everywhere given great satisfaction. This because I aim to give the best that the purchaser's money will build. If you buy a thirty-dollar canvas covered canoe you get the best that thirty dollars can buy. If you buy a two hundred dollar AA grade boat you get one worth that sum.

The luxury of one decade becomes the necessity of the next. Once the summer vacation was a luxury. Today, with our strenuous business life, it is a necessity, and there are few who do not plan at least a short vacation with a change of scene and the outlay of more or less money to make that vacation pleasant.

Away then from workshop and office, away to the green fields or greener wildwood, to the stream where the rapids roar or the long reaches of still water flow between overhanging boughs, or where the lakelet spreads out in placid beauty between the hills. Did you ever stand on the bank of stream or lake and remark, "*If I only had a boat.*" In fairy tales here is where the Genii appear. In real life the speaker gets left if he has been so unwise or careless as not to have provided for this very emergency before leaving home. In no way can he provide for it in so satisfactory a manner as by having brought with him a RUSHTON boat or canoe.

These boats are the product of long years of labor spent in designing models, selecting and working material, and embody the best that can be found in each. If a model does not strike popular favor it is soon withdrawn and replaced by a later design. If popular it is retained. Long since, any material unsuited to the purpose was weeded out. Thus it occurs that ALL my boats are SELLERS. Select the one suited to your wants.

WEIGHTS—I have built several boats of less than fifteen pounds weight, and one of 9¾ pounds only. This one was used for about two years by "Nessmuk" and I am told is still in good condition. Such weights, however, are not practical for the average person, even if of light weight (Nessmuk weighed about 100 pounds), and any of my boats or canoes will be found light enough for all practical purposes. Bear in mind that I give *actual weight* where any is named in Catalogue.

In the following pages I endeavor to give you a clear description of such staple goods as I manufacture, and will supplement by letter any further information on request. In most cases it is best to make selections from Catalogue, particularly from April until September (my busy season), but if for any reason you cannot be suited with such boats as are named I will be pleased to correspond with you and arrange for special model or construction where either is practical. In short—IF YOU. DO NOT SEE WHAT YOU WANT ASK FOR IT.

SELECTION OF A BOAT.

When you wish to purchase a small Boat or Canoe take none but one of CEDAR planking. Whatever is second, Cedar is FIRST and by so many points of excellence that no other is worth serious consideration. Almost as light as cork, tough and everlasting, it so far outclasses everything else as to be in a class by itself.

HOW TO USE AND CARE FOR A BOAT.

It may not be amiss right here to say a few words to those unaccustomed to the use or care of light, fine boats and canoes. Don't avoid the fine, light boat because it is such. If you will but give it reasonable use and care it will do you good service and be much more satisfactory than the "any old thing," that, while costing less, is dear at any price.

If you transport your boat by rail—in a baggage car—help put it in the car, see that it is placed where no sharp corners of boxes or trunks will gouge a hole in it. Give the baggageman a quarter, ask him (pleasantly) to look after it, and be on hand to take it out of the car. If you have to transport it over a rough woods road on a wagon—DON'T. Pay some one a dollar, more or less, to carry it on his shoulders.

When you embark see that it rests entirely in the water, not half its length on shore, nor on stones or snags. When you get into it don't see how hard you can jump; don't see if you can kick a hole in it with hob-nailed shoes: probably you can. In fact, I will assure you that you can, and save you the trouble of trying. Step in the center of the boat—over the keel—sit down quietly, stay there. Many a life has been lost by "fooling around" in a boat. Never try to be "cute" just to scare the other fellow. You may be the worse scared of the two before you get out of the scrape. Don't TRY to change places in the boat with another person *unless you must.*

If I had to change places in a canoe with a companion, one of us would curl down in the bottom while the other, with a hand on either gunwale, would crawl over. *This is the only safe way in any canoe or small boat.* Keep off stones and snags as much as possible. When you land use equal care. If there is water inside your boat empty it out. If you make a temporary landing do not leave your boat half on shore and half in the water to pound in current or wind. Pull it on shore and leave it in the shade if you can. At permanent landings keep it under some sort of shelter when not in use. Do not leave it for days and weeks in the water or in the hot sun.

When the season is over clean it up and leave it in a moderately dry place under roof. After a few weeks look it over. If any nails are loosened, reclinch them. If it has had long and severe usage go over it as best you can with medium fine or half-worn sandpaper, and give it a coat of spar varnish. If it has had but moderate use and good care it will not need revarnishing oftener than once in two or three years.

Take the same proper care of it as you do of your other belongings, and be one of the considerable number who write me each year how their boat, bought from me ten, fifteen, yes, often *twenty* or more years ago is still in good condition.

4

PLEASURE BOATS—Model, Material, Construction.

Models—The value of a boat depends largely on its model, and the model must be adapted to the purpose for which it is intended. A boat for ladies' and children's use should be broad and flat on the bottom, safety being the prime, and speed the secondary, consideration. For the expert boatman more dead rise and finer lines give a faster boat and is safe enough for him. However, all steady, safe boats are not slow. Nor are all cranky boats fast. I have tried (for 29 years) to obtain the best possible results from given dimensions, viz: the fastest safe boat and the safest fast boat. A further description of models will be found in the engravings and descriptions of individual boats.

Material—Do not confound our White Cedar, which grows only in the most Northern States and Canada, with the White Cedar of New Jersey and Virginia. The former is the lightest known wood of this or any country, that is suitable for planks for small craft. One cubic foot, air seasoned (not kiln-dried), weighing but *eighteen pounds*, while the so-called White Cedar of New Jersey and Virginia weighs 28 pounds.

The Northern Cedar is soft, tough and durable. You can give it a vast amount of hard usage with but little injury, and *time* makes little impression on it, as I have known the Cedar planking in a boat to be sound and perfect after twenty years' constant use every summer and having only such shelter winters as may be found in a woods camp.

Spanish Cedar, imported from the West Indies and Central America, has a more beautiful color, hence makes a finer looking craft, but it is neither so light nor tough as the White Cedar.

Black Cherry is the finest of all our native hard woods and the most costly. It is close grained and finishes very smooth, is of a reddish color that deepens and darkens with age. Mahogany, Oak, Ash, Spruce, etc., are too well known to require description here.

CONSTRUCTION—LAP STREAK.

For Twenty-Nine Years I have been a believer in and builder of lap streak boats. I believe it to be the very best and strongest system in use for light work. Witness the ten-pound Sairy Gamp, built for "Nessmuk," and the still lighter canoe built for and used by him for two seasons in Florida at a later date, and still in commission. It would be simply impossible to build to these light weights by any other system.

With each streak shaped and fitted for its particular place, and the edges lapped and firmly fastened together, it becomes in strength as one whole piece without the strain that attends warping into place broad streaks, neither does it depend entirely on the timbers to hold the planking together, as in carvel built boats.

Smooth Skin—I make Smooth Skin by beveling each streak to an edge inside and out, and at the curve or bilge working the streaks hollow and round from thicker material. It is then double clinch fastened on planking 1/4 inch or under in thickness, viz: nailed from both sides, the tack head always on the thin edge and the clinch in solid wood.

Square Stern Boats—Any of my pleasure boats will be built square stern, to order, for the extra cost as named in description of individual boats.

5

PLEASURE BOATS—GRADES.

GRADE AA. THIS GRADE BUILT ONLY TO ORDER.

MATERIAL—Selected oak keelson; stem and sternpost bent cherry. Planking and decks, selected Spanish cedar. Ribs, red elm. Gunwales, inwales and coaming, cherry. Stern seat of cherry or other fine wood; the other seats are caned unless otherwise stated in description of individual boat. Floor gratings, oak or cherry, or both combined. All exposed fastenings of copper or brass. Best grade linseed oil and spar varnish for finish. Brass, nickel-plated, stem bands, and fancy pattern seat braces.

CONSTRUCTION—Hull, SMOOTH SKIN. The joints are lapped from ½ to ¾ inch, and double clinch fastened throughout if ¼ inch planking. The bilge streaks are from thicker material than the other streaks, and are hollowed and rounded by hand. The ribs are clinch fastened (unless otherwise by special order), not only on the joints but at the center of the plank when below water line, this to prevent warping or bulging. The ribs are spaced from two to four inches, according to thickness of planking, and the ends are pocketed in the inwale, making a solid rail, and adding to both the strength and beauty of the boat. The decks are from 18 to 32 inches long (according to length of boat) and are made of strips, usually ⅜ inch wide by ½ inch deep, laid to follow gunwale line, and blind nailed to the deck timbers and to each other. The deck batten covers the joint made in the center, and a small coaming forms the finish at the inner end. The grating is made of narrow strips laid lengthwise of the boat and fastened to cross pieces skin fitted to the planking. The seat frames are made with double doweled joints.

FINISH—One coat filler, two of best spar varnish (on a hurry order, two coats best white shellac are used in place of the first coat of varnish.)

FITTINGS—Are named with each individual boat.

REMARKS—With the rich combination of colors in the natural woods, and elegant finish and furnishings, no craft can be more beautiful. Neither time nor money will be spared to put the greatest possible intrinsic value into it.

If any boat is given an individual description as to material, in whole or in part, (as Livery boat, Saranac or Indian), go by that description—otherwise by general description of grades.

6

PLEASURE BOATS—GRADES.

GRADE A.

MATERIAL—Selected oak keelson ; bent oak or elm stem and sternpost. Planking, selected Northern white cedar, except sheer streak, that of Spanish cedar. Ribs, red elm. Gunwales, inwales and coamings, cherry, ash, or oak. Decks and battens, Spanish cedar or cherry. Stern seat of cherry or other fine wood ; the other seats are caned unless otherwise stated in description of individual boat. Inside floor of basswood, or other suitable material. All exposed fastenings of copper or brass. Oil and varnish finish. Nickel plated stem bands and seat braces.

CONSTRUCTION—The same as Grade AA, EXCEPT a plain bottom board instead of grating.

FINISH—One coat linseed oil and two of best spar varnish, or, on a hurried job, two coats of shellac substituted for first coat of varnish.

FITTINGS—Will be named with each individual boat.

REMARKS—This grade is quite equal to Grade AA, in strength and durability, and is elegant in every respect.

GRADE B.

MATERIAL—The same as Grade A, except the various kinds of wood are of a trifle lower grade and stem bands and seat braces are not plated.

CONSTRUCTION—LAP STREAK, clinch fastened, otherwise like Grade A.

FINISH—The same as Grade A.

FITTINGS—Will be named with each individual boat.

GRADE C.

MATERIAL—Keelson and stems, oak. Planking, sound Northern white cedar. Ribs, red elm. Gunwales, ash ; inwales, seats, decks, battens, coamings and floor, of any suitable wood. All exposed fastenings of copper or brass. Brass stem bands reaching to above water line. Polished brass seat braces. Oil and varnish finish.

CONSTRUCTION—LAP STREAK, clinch fastened, ends of ribs pocketed in inwale, decks as in higher grades, seats plain wood.

FINISH—One coat linseed oil and two coats of best spar varnish, or shellac ·may be substituted for first coat of varnish.

FITTINGS—Will be named with each individual boat.

REMARKS—This is a thoroughly well made, well finished, up-to-date, every day, all-around boat ; one that I can guarantee in every respect. Well suited to livery use, and all other purposes where only a moderate outlay is desired.

If any boat is given an individual description as to material, in whole or in part (as Livery boat, Saranac or Indian), go by that description, otherwise by general description of grades.

7

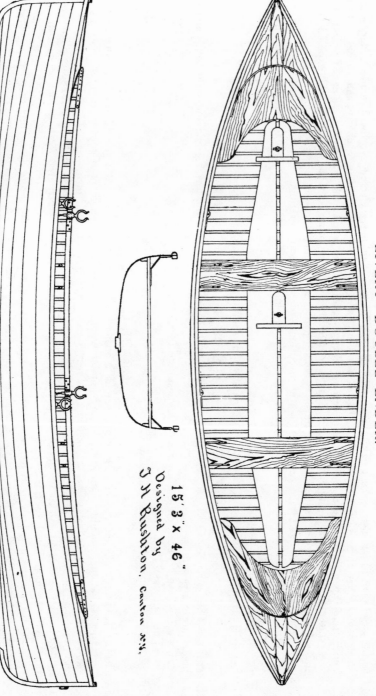

PLEASURE ROW BOATS—DESCRIPTION AND PRICES.

LIVERY—DOUBLE ENDER.

15' 3" x 46"

Designed by
J H Rushton, Canton N.Y.

8

PLEASURE ROW BOATS—Description and Prices.

LIVERY—DOUBLE ENDER. (See opposite page.)

This boat is designed and built to provide a very strong, durable, yet comparatively low priced boat for livery purposes. It is built in but one size, one grade. Dimensions and finish as shown.

MATERIAL—Keelson, oak; stems, elm; planking, sound white cedar; ribs, red elm; decks, ash; battens, white cedar; seats, ash; gunwales and inwales, ash; floor, basswood; all exposed fastenings, copper or brass.

CONSTRUCTION—Planking 5-16 inch thick, the usual lapstreak, clinch fastened. Ribs spaced 3 inches. Brass stem bands as in C grade boats.

FINISH—One coat linseed oil, two of spar varnish. When built to order will be painted any color, except white or vermilion, at same price.

FITTINGS—At prices here named will be one pair straight blade ash or spruce oars; one pair polished brass rowlocks, No. 1 oarlock with No. 4 socket.

PRICE, crated, F. O. B. here, $60.

Liberal discount on large orders.

LIVERY—SQUARE STERN. (See next page.)

This boat is in dimensions, material, construction, finish and fittings the same as the preceding boat. It differs ONLY in being square stern.

PRICE, crated, F. O. B. here, $65.

Liberal discount on large orders.

9

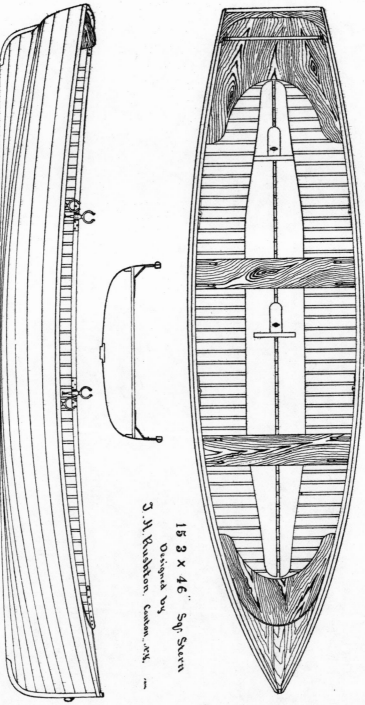

PLEASURE ROW BOATS—DESCRIPTION AND PRICES.

LIVERY—SQUARE STERN.

15 3 x 46" Sq. Stern

Designed by

J. H. Rushton, Canton, N.Y.

ADIRONDACK OR SARANAC LAKE BOAT.

STANDARD MAKE.

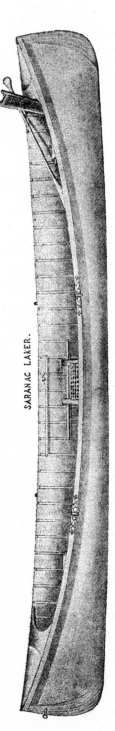

SARANAC LAKER.

STANDARD DIMENSIONS—Length, 16 feet; beam, 37 inches.

MATERIAL—Stems and knees, spruce or hackmatack; bottom, clear white pine or white cedar; planking and decks, clear white cedar; seat frames and gunwales, cherry. All fastenings, copper or brass. Brass strips on bottom and brass stem bands.

CONSTRUCTION—Stems and knees, natural crooks. Knees about ¾ x ⅜, spaced 4 inches. Planking ¼ inch thick. Smooth lap as in Grade A boats. Gunwales neatly rounded, except where sockets go on. Decks in narrow strips, not as shown here. Three cane bottom seats.

FINISH—One coat linseed oil, two of best spar varnish.

FITTINGS—Two pair sockets; 1 pair oarlocks No. 4, polished brass; 1 pair 8½ feet, square loom, hand made oars; 1 single blade maple paddle; cane back for stern seat; cane back and fixtures for middle seat, and carrying yoke. Notwithstanding its size, this boat can be safely built to weigh under 60 pounds.

PRICE, $100.00.

ALSO the same boat, EXCEPT built with elm ribs, steam bent, like my other row boats. Ribs spaced 3 inches, and with inwale as in other kinds. Fittings as above named.

PRICE, $90.00. This style construction is built only to order.

11

PLEASURE ROW BOATS—Description and Prices.

IDAHO   Lines of No. 3, View of No. 0.

PLEASURE ROW BOATS—Description and Prices.

IDAHO.

Number.	Length Feet.	Beam Inches.	Depth at Ends.	Depth Amidship.	Thickness of Planking.	Number of Seats.	PRICE Grade AA	PRICE Grade A.	PRICE Grade B.	PRICE Grade C.
1	20	40	25	15½	3/8	4	$190 00	$145 00	$105 00	$85 00
2	19	40	25	15½	3/8	4	180 00	140 00	100 00	80 00
3	18	40	25	15½	3/8	4	170 00	135 00	95 00	75 00
If built square stern						add	14 00	12 00	10 00	10 00
For copper tanks						"	9 00	9 00	9 00	9 00
For removable bulkheads in front of air tanks						"	4 50	4 50	4 00	4 00

At above named prices the fittings are :

GRADE AA—Brass stem bands and painter fastenings, flag pole tubes and plates, fancy pattern seat braces, No. 57 rudder braces, two pairs No. 1 rowlocks, all nickel plated. Two small sticks for flags, one wood rudder, two pairs best spruce spoon oars, two foot braces, one No. 1 chair seat.

GRADE A—All fittings the same as for Grade AA, *except* plain pattern seat braces.

GRADE B—Brass stem bands and painter fastenings, No. 58 rudder braces, seat braces, two pairs No. 1 rowlocks, all in polished brass. Two pairs spoon oars, two foot braces, rudder, one No. 2 chair seat.

GRADE C—Stem bands reaching from above water line ; painter fastenings, seat braces, No. 58 rudder braces, two pair No. 1 rowlocks, all in polished brass. Two pairs straight blade spruce oars, two foot braces and rudder.

Oars leathered with flange and to lap about four inches unless otherwise ordered.

13

PLEASURE ROW BOATS—DESCRIPTION AND PRICES.

FLORIDA. (No. 4, 17 x 42.)

PLEASURE ROW BOATS—DESCRIPTION AND PRICES.

FLORIDA.

Number.	Length Feet.	Beam Inches.	Depth at Ends.	Depth Amidship.	Thickness of Planking.	Number of Seats.	PRICE Grade AA.	PRICE Grade A.	PRICE Grade B.	PRICE Grade C.
4	17	42	25½	15¾	$\frac{5}{16}$	4	$165 00	$130 00	$95 00	$75 00
5	16	42	25½	15¾	¼	3	157 00	125 00	90 00	71 00
6	15	42	25½	15¾	¼	3	150 00	120 00	85 00	68 00
If built square stern --------------- add							14 00	12 00	10 00	10 00
For copper air tanks------------------ "							9 00	9 00	9 00	9 00
For removable bulkheads in front of air tanks--------- "							5 00	5 00	4 50	4 50

At above named prices the fittings are :

GRADE AA—Brass stem bands and painter fastenings, flag pole tubes and plates, fancy pattern seat braces, No. 57 rudder braces, two pairs No. 1 rowlocks, all nickel plated. Two small sticks for flags, one wood rudder, two pairs best spruce spoon oars, two foot braces, one No. 1 chair seat.

GRADE A—All fittings the same as for Grade AA, *except* plain pattern seat braces.

GRADE B—Brass stem bands and painter fastenings, No. 58 rudder braces, two pairs No. 1 rowlocks, all polished brass. Two pairs spoon oars, two foot braces, rudder and one No. 2 chair seat.

GRADE C—Stem bands reaching from above water line, painter fastenings, seat braces, No. 58 rudder braces, two pairs No. 2 rowlocks, all in polished brass. Two pairs spruce straight blade oars, two foot braces and rudder.

Oars leathered with flange and to lap about four inches unless otherwise ordered.

PLEASURE ROW BOATS—Description and Prices.

IOWA. (No. 8.)

PLEASURE ROW BOATS—Description and Prices.

IOWA.

Number.	Length Feet.	Beam Inches.	Depth at Ends	Depth Amidship.	Thickness of Planking.	Number of Seats.	PRICE Grade AA.	PRICE Grade A.	PRICE Grade B	PRICE Grade C.
6	15	36	23	14	1/4	3	$140 00	$110 00	$75 00	$64 00
7	14	36	23	14	1/4	3	135 00	105 00	70 00	59 00
8	13	36	23	14	1/4	3	130 00	100 00	65 00	54 00
If built square stern						add	12 00	11 00	10 00	10 00
For copper air tanks						"	8 50	8 50	8 50	8 50
For removable bulkheads in front of air tanks						"	4 50	4 50	4 00	4 00

At above named prices the fittings are:

GRADE AA—Brass stem bands and painter fastenings, flag pole tubes and plates; fancy pattern seat braces, No. 57 rudder braces, one pair No. 1 rowlocks, all nickel plated; two small sticks for flags, one wood rudder, one pair best spruce spoon oars, one foot brace and one No. 1 chair seat.

GRADE A—All fittings the same as Grade AA, *except* plain pattern seat braces.

GRADE B—Brass stem bands and painter fastenings; No. 58 rudder braces, seat braces, one pair No. 1 rowlocks, all polished brass; one pair spoon oars, one foot brace, rudder and one No. 2 chair seat.

GRADE C—Stem bands reaching from above water line; painter fastenings, seat braces, No. 58 rudder braces, one pair No. 1 rowlocks, all polished brass; one pair straight blade oars, one foot brace and rudder.

Oars leathered with flange and to lap about four inches unless otherwise ordered.

17

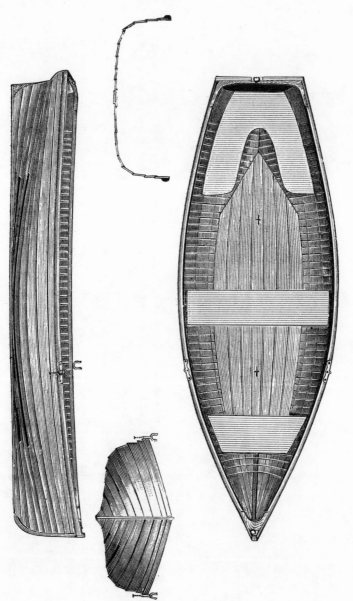

SQUARE STERN FISHING BOAT OR DINGHY.

(SEE NEXT PAGE.)

18

SQUARE STERN FISHING BOAT OR DINGHY.

Number.	Length Feet.	Beam Feet.	Thickness of Planking Inches.	Number of Seats.	PRICE Grade AA.	PRICE Grade A.	PRICE Grade B.	PRICE Grade C.
185	9	3	¼	3	$ 80 00	$ 60 00	$55 00	$45 00
190	10 ½	3 ½	¼	3	87 50	67 50	60 00	50 00
195	12	5/16	3	100 00	80 00	70 00	60 00
200	13 ½	4 ½	⅜	4	120 00	92 50	80 00	70 00
205	15	5	⅜	4	145 00	115 00	95	85 00

MATERIAL—The same as other row boats of like grade, *except* all wood seats in all grades. Ash in Grades B and C, and cherry or other fine wood in the higher grades.

CONSTRUCTION—The same as other row boats of like grades, *except* in place of decks, breast hooks and corner braces are used, and stern seat is shaped about as here shown. Inside floor 3 to 5 strips screwed to ribs.

FINISH—The same as other row boats of like grade.

FITTINGS—*At above named prices.* For No. 185 and No. 190 one pair of oars and one pair of rowlocks, one pair extra sockets to enable rowing from middle seat, one foot brace and rudder. For Nos. 195, 200, 205, two pairs oars, two pairs rowlocks, two foot braces and rudder. Rowlocks—pattern known as No. 5—nickel plated for Grades AA and A, polished brass for Grades B and C. These No. 5 rowlocks go on inside of gunwale (not as shown), leaving the gunwale smooth on the outside. (See cut, page 63.) Numbers 200 and 205 are only built to order.

OARS—Spoon blades for Grades AA and A. Straight blades for Grades B and C.

PLEASURE ROW BOATS—Description and Prices.

ISLANDER.

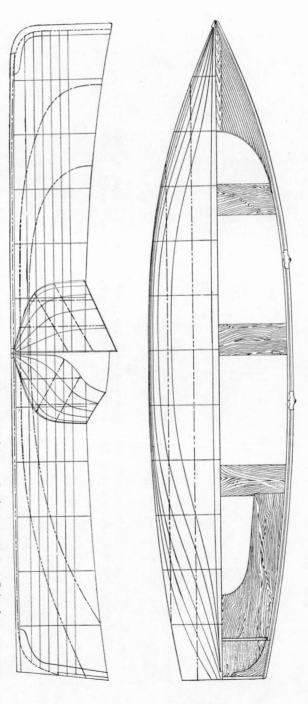

DIMENSIONS—Length, 18 feet; beam, 4 feet; depth, at bow 31 inches, amidship 24 inches, at stern 28 inches. Planking ⅜ inch thick, other materials in proportion. All wood seats in every grade as shown above, otherwise as per description pages.

PRICES—Grade AA, $250.00. Grade A, $210.00. Grade B, $180.00. Grade C, $150.00. Built only to order.

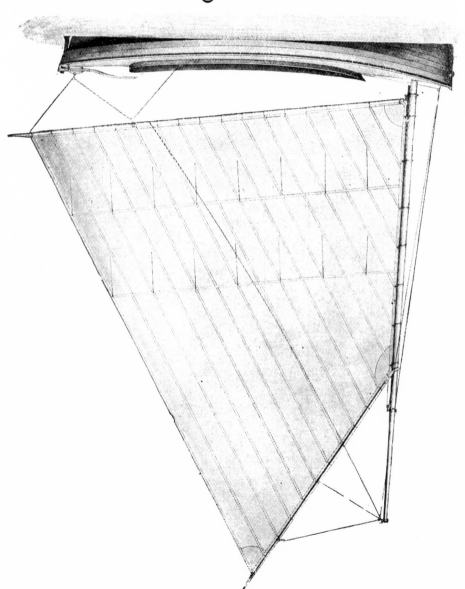

CAT BOAT.
15 x 5

SAIL PLAN.

(SEE NEXT PAGE.)

21

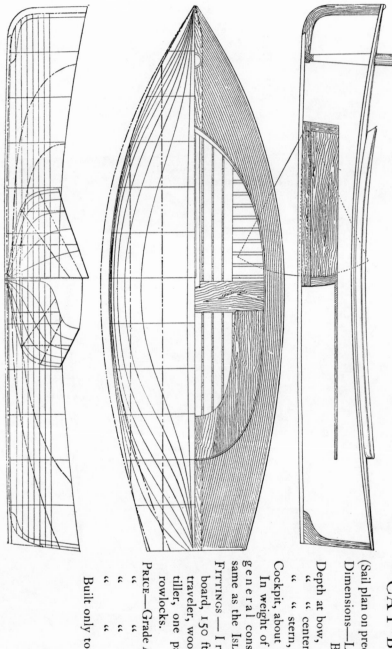

CAT BOAT.

(Sail plan on preceding page.)

Dimensions—Length, 15 ft.

" " Beam, 5 "

Depth at bow, 30 inches

" " center, 19 "

" " stern, 27 "

Cockpit, about 9x4 ft.

In weight of material and general construction the same as the ISLANDER.

FITTINGS — Iron centerboard, 150 ft. Gaff Rig, traveler, wood rudder and tiller, one pair oars and rowlocks.

PRICE—Grade AA, $275.00

" " A, 210.00

" " B, 185.00

" " C, 160.00

Built only to order.

COMBINATION ROW AND SAIL BOATS.

The one shown here is FLORIDA No. 6 (15 x 42), fitted with Gaff Rig No. 21 (75 feet), and No. 2 Radix Centerboard. A small after or mizzen sail and a main sail with shorter spars than the Gaff rig are preferred by some. Combination row and sail boats are now listed differently than here shown. (See tables.)

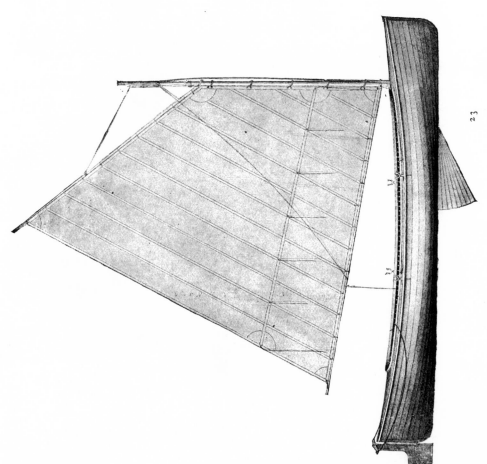

23

COMBINATION ROW AND SAIL BOATS.

The average man does not greatly admire a white ash or spruce breeze, and likes to have the wind blow his way. When it does he can hoist any old thing for a sail and take it easy. But the wind is often contrary, or at least, blows from the wrong direction. We therefore devise ways and means to still make it our servant. By use of Lee or Centerboard we make it serve our purpose, and by taking a zig-zag course across it (called tacking) may reach a point dead to windward of our present position. To accomplish this, however, we must take the wind well on the beam, and while it forces the boat ahead as we would have it, it also forces it bodily to leeward and tries to roll it over. It is readily understood then that with a boat entirely open on top but small sail area can be carried, else our lee rail goes under and we come to grief. Hence to give our boat increased sail carrying power we deck it along the sides as well as at the ends and around the cockpit thus formed bend in a low coaming. We call this a

Combination Row and Sail Boat, because it detracts little from its convenience or value as a row boat while making it a practical sail boat with more or less sail carrying power according to its beam and the skill of the sailor. As a further element of safety, air tanks or water tight bulkheads are provided for the ends, though they may be omitted at the option of the purchaser. When bulkheads are used the compartments thus formed may, by putting hatches through the decks or bulk-heads, be used for storage purposes, still remaining a fairly good substitute for air tanks.

LEE BOARDS OR CENTERBOARDS NECESSARY.

While the wind pressure against the sail tends to roll the boat over, it also forces the hull through the water to leeward. To overcome this so far as possible, we increase the resistance of the hull *in that direction* by use of a lee board or center-board. As the latter is more effective and can quite as well be used in these boats, we may omit further mention of the former here.

The centerboard being short and being placed nearly amidship, fairly maintains the *center* of resistance of the hull while largely increasing that resistance. If, now, our sail area is too far forward, the wind pushes the bow of the boat to leeward, and a constant "Lee Helm," as it is called, is required. On the other hand, if the sail area is too far aft it is the stern of the boat that is pushed around, and a constant "Weather Helm" is required. Under definition of "Lee Helm," DIXON KEMP says: "The helm put to leeward to keep a vessel to or by the wind, synonymous with slack helm. If the center of effort of the sails is much forward of the center of lateral resistance, the vessel will have a tendency to fall off, and will require the helm to be put to leeward to keep her close to the wind. The tendency can be checked by reducing the head sail, or by hardening in the sheets of the after sail and easing the sheets of the head sail."

COMBINATION ROW AND SAIL BOATS.

"Weather Helm—The helm or tiller hauled to windward when a vessel, owing to too much aftersail, has an inclination to fly up in the wind. If the center of effort of the sails is much abaft the center of lateral resistance a vessel will require a weather helm to keep her out of the wind. The tendency to fly up in the wind can be remedied by reducing the aftersail, or setting more head sail, or by easing the main sheet. However, all vessels should carry a little weather helm."

By shifting the position of the centerboard either way as far as it will go and by loading our boat on an even keel or down a little by the stern, we shift the center of resistance fore and aft to some extent and thereby are able to use a considerable number of combination of rigs. In naming suitable rigs for each individual boat it is contemplated placing the after end of the centerboard from six inches forward to six inches aft the center of the boat and of loading the craft from an even keel to two inches down by the stern.

A further increase in the variety of rigs that can be used in any boat is obtained by varying the center of effort a little as compared with the center of resistance, which should be not more than twelve nor less than six inches *forward*.

SEATING—These COMBINATION ROW AND SAIL BOATS will be seated the same as the regular rowboat of the same size and grade, or, as nearly so as will allow the centerboard to be placed in proper position.

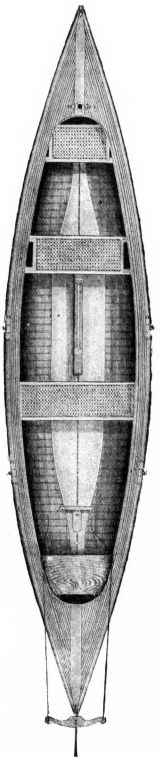

This view shows deck and interior of Florida No. 4, 17 x 42, Grade B, when decked as a Combination Row and Sail Boat.

COMBINATION ROW AND SAIL BOAT.

IDAHO. (See pages 12–13.)

Number.	Grade.	Centerboard.	Rigs.	Area.	Price.	Number.	Grade.	Centerboard.	Rigs.	Area.	Price.
0	AA	No. 2 Radix.	43 and 26	112 Sq. Ft.	$279 00	0	B	No. 2 Radix.	43 and 26	112 Sq. Ft.	$189 00
1	"	" 2 "	43 " 26	" " "	269 00	1	"	" 2 "	43 " 26	" " "	184 00
2	"	" 2 "	43 " 26	" " "	259 00	2	"	" 2 "	43 " 26	" " "	179 00
3	"	" 2 "	42 " 35	100 " "	248 00	3	"	" 2 "	42 " 35	100 " "	173 00
0	A	No. 2 Radix.	43 and 26	112 Sq. Ft.	$229 00	0	C	No. 2 Radix.	43 and 26	112 Sq. Ft.	$164 00
1	"	" 2 "	43 " 26	" " "	224 00	1	"	" 2 "	43 " 26	" " "	159 00
2	"	" 2 "	43 " 26	" " "	219 00	2	"	" 2 "	43 " 26	" " "	154 00
3	"	" 2 "	42 " 35	100 " "	213 00	3	"	" 2 "	42 " 35	100 " "	148 00

At above named prices air tanks are included, also the regular rowboat outfit for same size and grade, using No. 2 rowlocks.

COMBINATION ROW AND SAIL BOAT.

FLORIDA. (See pages 14–15.)

Number.	Grade.	Centerboard.	Rigs.	Area.	Price.	Number.	Grade.	Centerboard.	Rigs.	Area.	Price.
4	AA	No. 2 Radix.	39 and 35	120 Sq. Ft.	$245 00	4	B	No. 2 Radix.	39 and 35	120 Sq. Ft.	$175 00
5	"	" 2 "	39 " 25	110 " "	235 00	5	"	" 2 "	39 " 25	110 " "	168 00
6	"	" 2 "	39 " 1	103 " "	223 00	6	"	" 2 "	39 " 1	103 " "	158 00
4	A	No. 2 Radix.	39 and 35	120 Sq. Ft.	$210 00	4	C	No. 2 Radix.	39 and 35	120 Sq. Ft.	$150 00
5	"	" 2 "	39 " 25	110 " "	203 00	5	"	" 2 "	39 " 25	110 " "	144 00
6	"	" 2 "	39 " 1	103 " "	193 00	6	"	" 2 "	39 " 1	103 " "	136 00

OUTFIT THE SAME AS FOR IDAHO

COMBINATION ROW AND SAIL BOAT.

IOWA. (See pages 16–17.)

Number.	Grade.	Centerboard.	Rigs.	Area.	Price.
6	AA	No. 1 Radix.	38 and 25	95 Sq. Ft.	$210 00
7	"	" 1 "	29 " 1	88 " "	200 00
8	"	" 1 "	28 " 1	73 " "	190 00
6	A	No. 1 Radix.	38 and 25	95 Sq. Ft.	$180 00
7	"	" 1 "	29 " 1	88 " "	170 00
8	"	" 1 "	28 " 1	73 " "	160 00

Number.	Grade.	Centerboard.	Rigs.	Area.	Price.
6	B	No. 1 Radix.	38 and 25	95 Sq. Ft.	$145 00
7	"	" 1 "	29 " 1	88 " "	135 00
8	"	" 1 "	28 " 1	73 " "	128 00
6	C	No. 1 Radix.	38 and 25	95 Sq. Ft.	$125 00
7	"	" 1 "	29 " 1	88 " "	117 00
8	"	" 1 "	28 " 1	73 " "	110 00

At above named prices air tanks are included, also the regular rowboat outfit for the same size and grade, using No. 2 rowlocks.

SQUARE STERN FISHING BOAT OR DINGHY.

FINISHED AND FITTED AS A COMBINATION ROW AND SAIL BOAT. (See pages 18–19.)

Number.	Grade.	Centerboard.	Rig No.	Area.	Price.
185	AA	No. 1 Radix.	18	40 Sq. Ft.	$130 00
190	"	" 1 "	20	60 " "	140 00
195	"	" 2 "	20	60 " "	160 00
200	"	" 2 "	22	100 " "	195 00
205	"	" 3 "	24	150 " "	240 00
185	A	No. 1 Radix.	18	40 Sq. Ft.	$110 00
190	"	" 1 "	20	60 " "	120 00
195	"	" 2 "	20	60 " "	140 00
200	"	" 2 "	22	100 " "	165 00
205	"	" 3 "	24	150 " "	200 00

Number.	Grade.	Centerboard.	Rig No.	Area.	Price.
185	B	No. 1 Radix.	18	40 Sq Ft.	$105 00
190	"	" 1 "	20	60 " "	110 00
195	"	" 2 "	20	60 " "	130 00
200	"	" 2 "	22	100 " "	150 00
205	"	" 3 "	24	150 " "	180 00
185	C	No. 1 Radix.	18	40 Sq. Ft.	$ 95 00
190	"	" 1 "	20	60 " "	100 00
195	"	" 2 "	20	60 " "	120 00
200	"	" 2 "	22	100 " "	140 00
205	"	" 3 "	24	150 " "	165 00

At above named prices air tanks are included, also the regular rowboat outfit for same size and grade, using No. 2 rowlocks,

PADDLING CANOES. DECKING, FINISH, Etc.

As I make several styles of decking for these canoes, it becomes necessary to designate each in such a manner as will not be confusing to the reader. I will therefore designate them as Styles A, B, C and D.

DESCRIPTION.

STYLE A.—(As shown on page 41.) Very short deck, a single piece of wood 6 to 12 inches long, according to length and weight of boat.

STYLE B.—(As shown on page 37.) Decks from 18 to 26 inches long, according to size of boat, made of strips about ⅜ inch thick by ½ inch deep, laid to follow gunwale line and blind nailed to deck beams and to each other. Proper finish is made by putting a thin batten over the center seam and by bending in a low coaming at inner ends of decks. This is the style most in use.

STYLE C —(As shown here.) Bow deck 24 inches long, stern deck 24 inches, deck at each side 2 inches. Coaming about 1 inch high above deck, thus forming a cockpit with oval shaped ends and varying in length according to the length of the canoe, and in width from about 20 to 24 inches in the various canoes. Decking and battens the same as in style B. No seats. This style deck built to order only.

STYLE D.—(Not illustrated.) Each individual canoe to be decked to make a cockpit just one-half the entire length of the canoe by from 18 to 20 inches wide with oval ends and placed at about equal distance from either end, leaving the cockpit from 5¼ feet in a 10½ ft. canoe, to 8½ feet in a 17 ft. one. Coaming and battens as in Style C. No seats. This style deck built to order only.

28

WAR CANOE.

DIMENSIONS, 30 x 50 x 36 x 22.

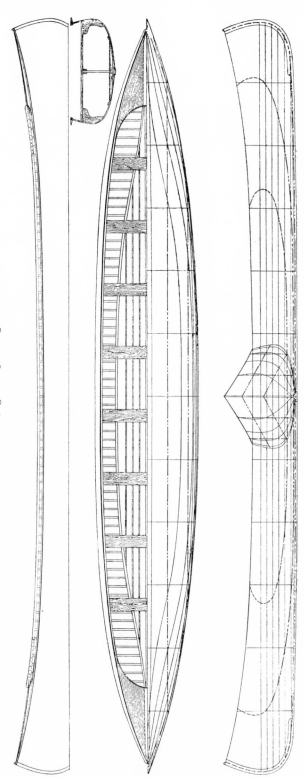

All planking white cedar, white cedar decks, oak keel, stems and thwarts. Planking ⅜ inch; all other material in proper proportion. In general construction like grade A canoes. Fitted for crew of 17 men. Outfit 17 single blade paddles. Price, F. O. B., $200.00. Built to order only.

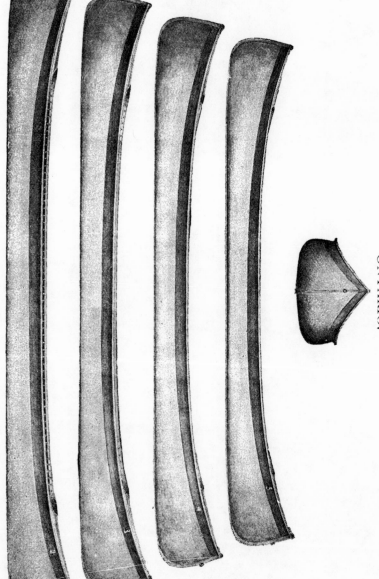

CANADIAN MODEL CANOES.
ONTARIO.

CANADIAN MODEL CANOES.

ONTARIO.

SEATING.—Either grade, decks style A or B, length 14 ft. or less, have each two seats. If length is 15 ft. or over each has three seats.

Either grade, any length, decks style C or D has no seats.

The ONTARIO Canoe measures about 19 in. depth at ends, and 12 in. amidship.

Number.	Length.	Beam.	Grade.	A	B	C	D
						STYLE OF DECKING.	
3	18 Feet	32 inches	AA	$92 00	$94 00	$102 00	$110 00
3	" "	" "	A	65 00	67 00	67 00	82 00
4	17 "	31 "	AA	88 00	90 00	97 00	104 50
4	" "	" "	A	61 00	63 00	70 00	77 50
5	16 "	30 "	AA	85 00	87 00	94 00	101 50
5	" "	" "	A	59 00	61 00	68 00	75 50
6	15 "	" "	AA	82 00	84 00	91 00	97 00
6	" "	" "	A	57 00	59 00	66 00	72 00
7	14 "	" "	AA	77 00	79 00	86 00	91 50
7	" "	" "	A	53 00	55 00	62 00	67 50
8	13 "	28 "	AA	73 00	75 00	82 00	86 50
8	" "	" "	A	50 00	52 00	59 00	63 50

Two single blade paddles constitute the outfit for each canoe. All else *extra*.

CANADIAN MODEL CANOES—IGO.

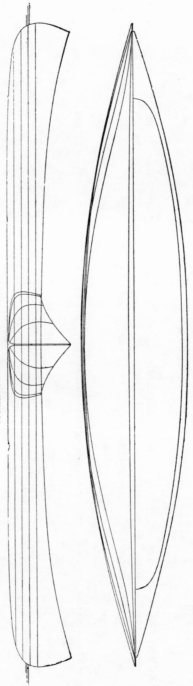

Number 6.

TAKEN FROM WORKING DRAWINGS.

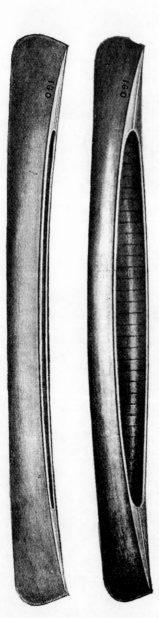

Number 6.

TAKEN FROM PHOTOGRAPH.

32

CANADIAN MODEL CANOES.

IGO.

The IGO canoe measures about 18 inches in depth at ends and 10½ inches amidship. It is very flat on the bottom, fine lines fore and aft, is very stiff and a swift, easy paddler. As it gets its full amidship bearing on very little draft, it is at its best with a medium load, say two or three persons.

SEATING.—Either grade, decks style A or B, length 14 feet or less, have two seats. If length is 15 feet or over, each has three seats. Either grade, any length, decks style C or D, has no seats.

Number.	Length.	Beam.	Grade.	STYLE OF DECKING.			
				A	B	C	D
4	17 Feet	31 Inches	AA	$88 00	$90 00	$97 00	$104 50
4	17 "	31 "	A	61 00	63 00	70 00	77 50
5	16 "	30 "	AA	85 00	87 00	94 00	101 50
5	16 "	30 "	A	59 00	61 00	68 00	75 50
6	15 "	30 "	AA	82 00	84 00	91 00	97 00
6	15 "	30 "	A	57 00	59 00	66 00	72 00
7	14 "	30 "	AA	77 00	79 00	86 00	91 50
7	14 "	30 "	A	53 00	55 00	62 00	67 50

At above named prices the fittings for either grade, any style deck, will be two single blade paddles.

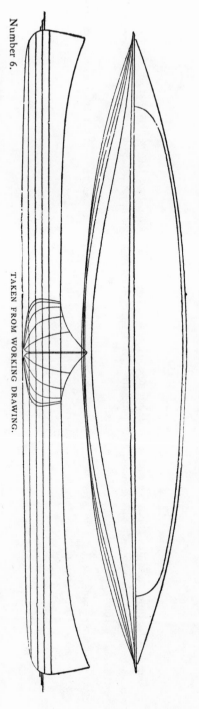

Number 6.

TAKEN FROM WORKING DRAWING.

Number 6.

TAKEN FROM PHOTOGRAPH.

CANADIAN MODEL CANOES.

UGO.

The UGO canoe measures about 18 inches in depth at ends and 11 inches amidship. It has moderate dead rise, quick bilge, fine lines, carries a heavy load with wonderful stiffness and is swift and easy under paddle.

SEATING—Either grade, decks style A or B, length 14 feet or less, have each two seats. If length is 15 feet or over, each has three seats. Either grade, any length, decks style C or D, has no seats.

Number.	Length.	Beam.	Grade.	STYLE OF DECKING.			
				A	B	C	D
4	17 Feet	30 Inches	AA	$88 00	$90 00	$97 00	$104 50
4	17 "	30 "	A	61 00	63 00	70 00	77 50
5	16 "	30 "	AA	85 00	87 00	94 00	101 50
5	16 "	30 "	A	59 00	61 00	68 00	75 50
6	15 "	30 "	AA	82 00	84 00	91 00	97 00
6	15 "	30 "	A	57 00	59 00	66 00	72 00
7	14 "	30 "	AA	77 00	79 00	86 00	91 50
7	14 "	30 "	A	53 00	55 00	62 00	67 50

At above named prices the fittings for either grade, any style deck, will be two single blade paddles.

35

CANADIAN MODEL LIGHT PADDLING CANOES.

ARKANSAW TRAVELER.

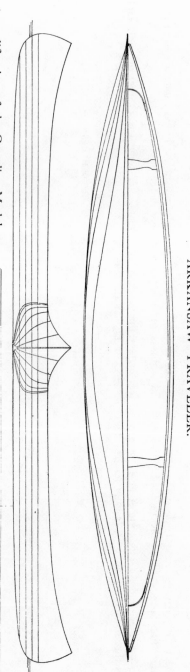

A modification of the Canadian Model combining to a marked degree fine lines, ease under paddle, speed, safety and stiffness. Of somewhat lighter construction than my other Canadian Models, they will rival the Birch Bark in weight and speed, while far more staunch, seaworthy and durable. Where the style of decking is A or B, two thwarts will be put in each instead of seats. In styles C and D no seats at list price, but they may be added as EXTRA. Two single blade paddles will complete the outfit. Weight 40 pounds and upward, according to size and style of decking. Only "A" style decks kept in stock.

Number.	Length.	Beam.	Grade.	STYLE OF DECKING.			
				A	B	C	D
4	17 Ft.	28 In.	AA	$78 00	$80 00	$87 00	$94 00
			A	$56 00	$58 00	$65 00	$72 00
5	16 Ft.	28 In.	AA	$75 00	$77 00	$84 00	$91 00
			A	$54 00	$56 00	$63 00	$70 00
6	15 Ft.	28 In.	AA	$72 00	$74 00	$81 00	$87 00
			A	$52 00	$54 00	$61 00	$67 00
7	14 Ft.	28 In.	AA	$69 00	$71 00	$78 00	$83 00
			A	$50 00	$52 00	$59 00	$64 00

PADDLING CANOES—VAUX AND VAUX, JR.

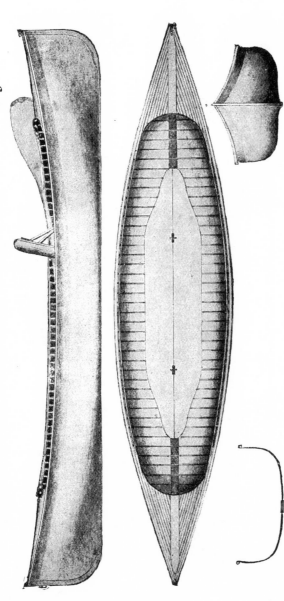

	Length.	Beam.	Depth at Ends.	Depth at Center.	Grade.	STYLE OF DECKING.			
						A	B	C	D
Vaux	10½ Feet	26 Inches	16 Inches	10½ Inches	AA	$75 00	$76 50	$83 50	$87 50
	" "	" "	" "	" "	A	36 00	37 50	44 50	49 00
Vaux, Jr.	11½ Feet	26 Inches	16 Inches	10½ Inches	AA	$83 50	$85 00	$92 00	$94 50
	" "	" "	" "	" "	A	41 00	42 50	49 50	56 50

Built only in Grades AA and A; ¼ in. planking, no fixed seats, otherwise in general construction like rowboats of same grade.

FITTINGS—For either grade are one double blade paddle, with drip cups; one ash folding seat.

37

PADDLING CANOES—HURON.

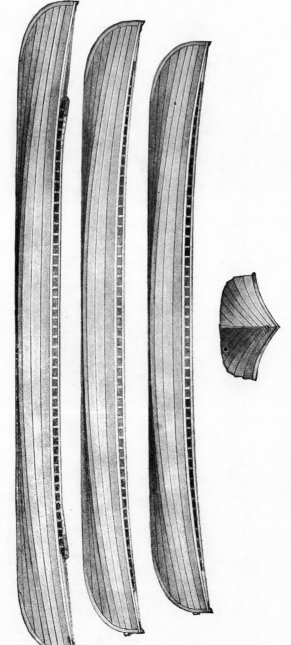

Number.	Length.	Beam.	Depth at Ends.	Depth at Center	Grade	STYLE OF DECKING.	
						A	B
5	16 Feet	30 Inches	18 Inches	11 Inches	C	$40 00	$42 00
6	15 "	" "	" "	" "	"	38 00	40 00
7	14 "	" "	" "	" "	"	36 00	38 00

Material, construction and finish, the same as Grade C rowboats. Ribs spaced 3 inches. Two seats. Outfit—Two single blade paddles.

PADDLING CANOES—ST. REGIS.

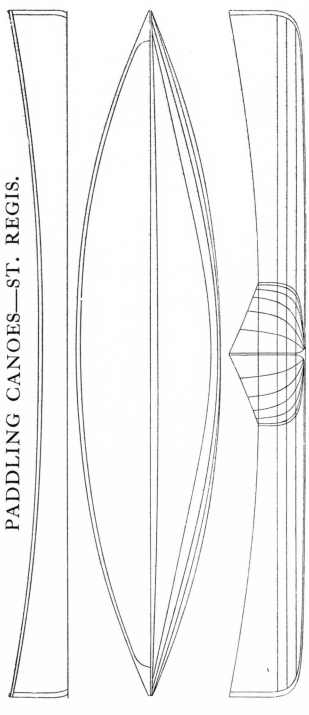

DIMENSIONS—Length, 12 feet; beam, 30 inches; depth at ends, 18 inches; depth amidship, 11 inches; weight about 40 pounds; carrying capacity, one or two persons and baggage.

Special Construction—viz.: Short decks. No seats.*

General Construction—Otherwise than above named, it is in material and construction the same as rowboats of similar grade.

BUILT only in Grades B and C. Style A decking.

PRICES—Grade B, $36.00. Grade C, $33.00.

At above named prices the fittings for either grade are—1 ash folding seat; 1 double-blade paddle, with drip cups.

*In canoes so small as Nessmuk, Bucktail, Vaux, Vaux Jr., and St. Regis, the weight of the paddler should be low down, and as his position may have to be changed, according as he has a companion or baggage, or neither, it is thought best to furnish them WITHOUT SEATS, leaving the canoeist to use a rug, cushion or folding seat, as suits him best.

39

PADDLING CANOES—BUCKTAIL.

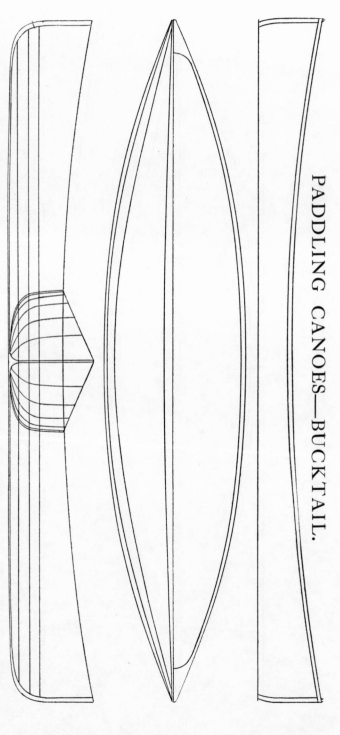

DIMENSIONS—Length, 10½ feet; beam, 26 inches; depth at ends, 16 inches; depth amidships, 10½ inches; thickness of planking, ¼ inch; decks about 10 inches long; no seats; weight, 30 to 35 pounds.

This canoe is a companion to the VAUX, being the same size and model. Very popular with the boys.

Built only in Grades B and C. Style A decking.

PRICES—Grade B, $31.00. Grade C, $27.50.

At the above named prices fittings for either grade are—1 ash folding seat; 1 double-blade paddle, with drip cups.

40

FEATHER-WEIGHT CANOES.

NESSMUK.

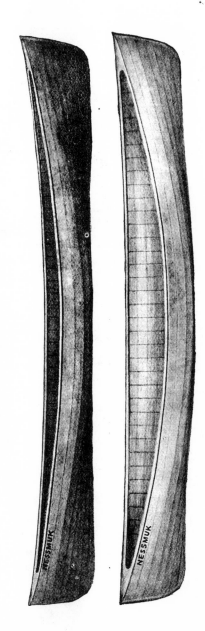

DIMENSIONS—Length, 10 ½ feet; beam, 27 inches; depth at ends, 15 inches; depth amidships, 9 inches; weight, about 18 to 22 pounds.

MATERIAL—Keel and stems, oak; planking, white cedar, 3-16 inch thick; gunwales and inwales, spruce; decks, white cedar; ribs, red elm.

CONSTRUCTION—Lapstreak; ribs very light and spaced 3 inches; very short decks; no inside floor.

FITTINGS—1 ash folding seat; 1 double-blade paddle, fitted with drip cups.

PRICE—$27.50.

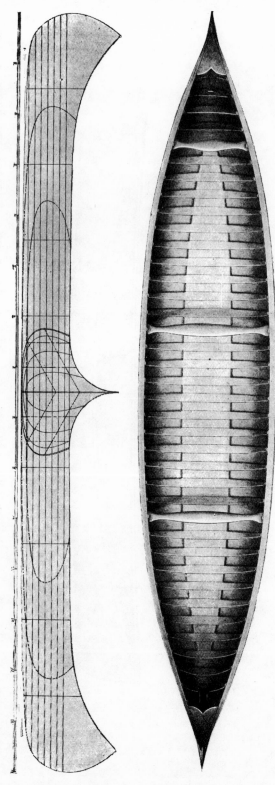

INDIAN.

Indian Model.—All Cedar Canoe. All white cedar except stems, gunwales and shoe.

Dimensions—Length, 15 feet; beam, 32 inches; depth at center, 12 inches; depth at ends, 24 inches; *weight only 47 pounds.*

Material—Ribs, planking, thwarts and decks, white cedar; stems, oak or elm; gunwales, cherry; stembands, brass.

Construction—Cedar ribs, 5-16 inch thick, 2 inches wide on bottom, tapering to 1¼ inch at gunwale, spaced 2 inches apart and filled in close between (on bottom) with 5-16 inch cedar, forming solid floor. Planking, 3-16 inch thick, put on smooth lap except center seam, which is a square seam covered by thin oak shoe. Clinch fastened throughout. Gunwales shaped like those of the Canadian models, but lighter and rounded a trifle on outer edge. Short decks, three thwarts, no inwales, 5-16 inch half oval stem bands. Finish, oil and varnish.

Fittings—Two single blade maple paddles. Price, $65.00.

42

CANVAS COVERED CEDAR CANOES.

If you will look over the back numbers of "Forest and Stream," away back in the Seventies, you will find me the pioneer builder of light cedar boats. From the few models in light hunting boats to the greatest variety of small craft ever offered by any one builder, has been the steady, healthy growth of more than a quarter of a century, and the designs and models of to-day are the results of long years of experiment and experience, to meet the varying conditions of use and the wishes of purchasers, many of whom have aided by their suggestions, although the designs and models have almost without exception been prepared in my shop by my own hand or under my direct supervision.

Other builders have followed, copying, imitating my work in a clumsy way as best they could, even in some cases illustrating their catalogues with cuts that could only have been produced by sending their engraver a page from my catalogue to copy. If "imitation is the sincerest flattery," I surely have received ample compensation.

I am a staunch believer in the Cedar Canoe without the canvas cover, and no less so now than heretofore, but I cater to the wishes of many, and among the number are those who prefer the canvas covering.

To the several builders of this class of work in the "Pine Tree State" belongs most of what credit there is in the production up to nearly the present time. I say this most willingly, although I cannot concede their claims to the superiority of the canvas covered vs. all wood canoes. I have built too many thousand all wood boats, have received too many hundreds of complimentary letters from those who have used them, to place them second to anything else.

WHAT I HAVE ALREADY DONE IN CANVAS COVERED CANOES.

The seasons of 1900 and 1901 were mostly spent in designing and experimental work, with no very considerable sales and with no attempt on my part to push this style of craft. Toward the close of the season of 1901, having perfected what I then believed to be the finest model canoe ever built, I said in my 1902 catalogue : "I have hired a skilled builder from Maine, a man with fourteen years' experience on this class of work, to superintend the construction. I will put with his, my own experience in designing and building *first-class goods* for the past *twenty-eight years* and together we expect to give you *better models* and *better goods* than you can obtain elsewhere *for the same money.*"

So well did we hew to the line thus drawn, that during the past season not half my orders could be filled, although I largely increased my working force and built more than double the intended number.

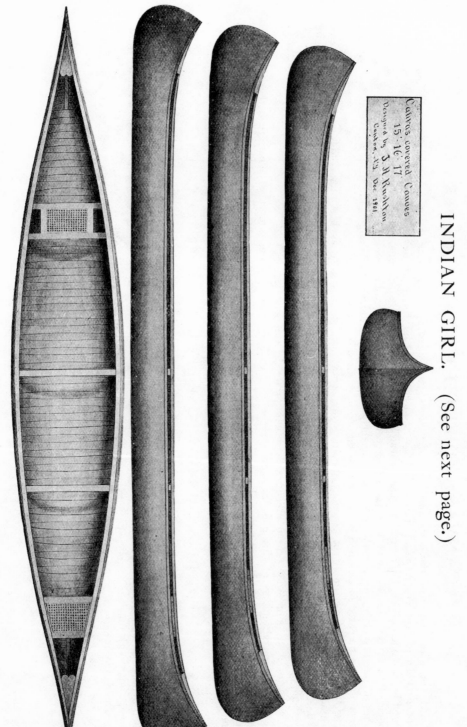

INDIAN GIRL. (See next page.)

Canvas covered Canoes
15', 16', 17'
Designed by J. H. Rushton
Canton, N.Y. Dec. 1901.

44

CANVAS COVERED CEDAR CANOES—INDIAN.

DIMENSIONS—Length, 15 feet; beam, 32 inches; depth at center, 12 inches; depth at ends, 24 inches. Weight, 59 to 65 pounds.

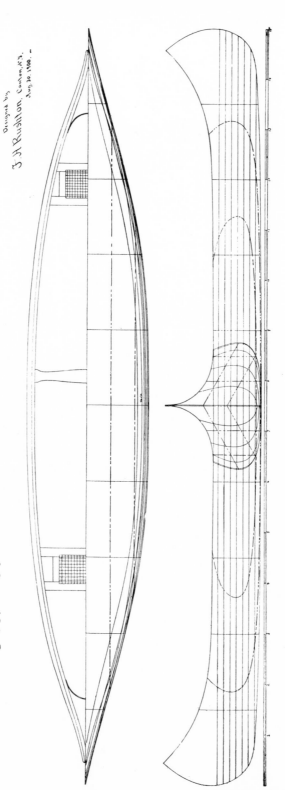

15'x31'
Canvas Canoe.
Designed by
J. H. Rushton, Canton, N.Y.
Aug. 30. 1900.

PRICE—Canoe only—Grade A, $40.00; Grade B, $32.00. For prices of extras, packing, etc., see table, page 47.

CANVAS COVERED CEDAR CANOES.

Models as shown on pages 44 and 45.

In 1902 two models were used and the canoes designated as "Indian" and "Indian Girl," the former being built in one length only, viz., 15 feet, the latter in three, viz., 15, 16 and 17 feet.

Indian Girl Model.—Built in four sizes, viz., 15, 16, 17 and 18 feet (see table of dimensions, weights and prices). This is, beyond a doubt, the most attractive canoe model ever offered. With three inches less sheer than "Indian," finer lines at bow and stern, yet with nearly the same flat floor amidship, it looks more graceful on the water, is a faster and easier paddler, while lacking nothing in stiffness or load carrying power.

Indian Model.—Built in one size only, viz.; length, 15 feet; beam, 32 inches; depth amidship, 12 inches; depth at bow and stern, 24 inches. All are outside measurements. Very flat on bottom, with rather full water lines. A very staunch canoe and very attractive where the greatest practical sheer is desired.

Grades.—Each model and size will be built in two grades called A and B.

GENERAL DESCRIPTION.

Grade A—*Material.*—Elm stems, steam bent; clear white cedar ribs and planking; cherry or oak inwales and gunwales; cherry decks, thwarts and seat frames; cane seats; ash gratings; polished brass stem bands, No. 10 duck. All exposed fastenings copper or brass.

Construction.—Ribs, 2 x 5-16 at bottom, tapering to 1¼ x 5-16 at inwale, spaced two inches apart. Planking 3-16 inch thick, square seam, clinch fastened to ribs. Inwales rabbeted for planking and pocketed for the ends of the ribs. Gunwales shaped the same as in the all wood canoes Ontario, Igo, &c. This style of gunwale gives vastly superior strength and beauty over any other method of construction. A grating (not shown in cut) composed of six light ash strips fastened to skin-fitted thwartship timbers completes the woodwork. No outside keel, except as an extra.

Height of Seats—The stern seat is placed just below the inwales, the forward seat about four inches lower.

Finish—On the canvas, two coats of special filling, two of color and one of varnish. On the exposed wood, one coat of linseed oil and two of best spar varnish.

Colors.—The prevailing color for stock goods will be *moss green.* Other ordinary colors furnished at the same price, but white or fancy colors, or striping or lettering will be charged extra.

CANVAS COVERED CEDAR CANOES.

Grade B—*Material*—Elm stems; sound white cedar ribs and planking. Inwales, covering strips, thwarts and seat frames of ash. No. 10 duck; caned seats; polished brass stembands. All exposed fastenings of copper or brass.

Construction—Stems, ribs and planking the same as in Grade A. The gunwales or top finish will be a substantial inwale to which the ends of the ribs are fastened, a thin strip of wood on the outside over the canvas and another on top, covering the otherwise exposed ends of the ribs and edge of planking and canvas, and making a proper finish. While this method is neither so strong nor handsome as the Grade A, it is the method employed by all other builders and seems to be satisfactory in medium priced canoes. No inside grating or outside keel except as an extra. In other respects the construction will be the same as Grade A.

Finish—On the canvas, two coats of special filling, two of color and one of varnish. On the exposed wood, one coat of linseed oil and two of best spar varnish.

Colors—The prevailing color for stock goods will be *moss green*. Other ordinary colors furnished at the same price, but white or fancy colors, or striping or lettering will be charged extra.

INDIAN GIRL.

No.	Length.	Beam.	Depth at Center.	Depth at End	Weight Grade A	Price Grade A	Weight Grade B	Price Grade B
1	15 ft.	32 in.	12 in.	21 in.	58 to 62	$38.00	56 to 60	$30.00
2	16 "	32½ "	12 "	21 "	60 " 66	39.00	58 " 64	31.00
3	17 "	33 "	12 "	21 "	65 " 75	40.00	60 " 66	32.00
4	18 "	33½ "	12 "	21 "	75 " 85	43.00	70 " 80	34.00

At above named prices no fittings are included and all packing for shipment is extra.

Extras—All decking other than standard length (about 15 inches) costs extra. The decks are put in place before the canvas goes on, therefore *any change*, however little, means extra cost and delay in shipment.

Ash decks, as in Grade B, if over 15 in. up to 30 in., $5.00 Lettering—Name painted, plain letters, both sides of
Cherry "   "   A, "   "   "   "   6.00   canoe, - - - - - - 1.00
Oak outside keel, not exceeding 1 inch deep, - - 1.50 Single blade Maple paddles, 4½ to 5½ ft., each, - 1.50
Colors—White or fancy colors or striping, from $2.00 up Grating for Grade B, - - - - - 1.00
Crating for shipment, - - - - $1.00 Packing in Burlap and Excelsior, - - $1.50
                    Both for same canoe, - - $2.50

Other fittings as per regular lists, and all changes in construction must be the subject of correspondence.

47

CRUISING SAILING CANOES.

VESPER MODEL.—Length, 16 feet; beam, 30 inches; depth at bow, 19 inches; at center, 11 inches; at stern, 16 inches.

MATERIAL.—Oak keel; Hackmatack stem and stern post, natural crook; ¼ inch white cedar planking except sheer streak; sheer streak, Spanish cedar; deck and hatches, mahogany; ribs, red elm; coaming, cherry; gunwales, oak or cherry; bulkheads and deck timbers, cedar; inside floor, basswood; all metal work copper or brass; finish, oil and best spar varnish.

CONSTRUCTION.—Smooth lap, clinch fastened hull, ribs spaced 2 inches, deck timbers spaced 6 inches; bulkheads 6½ feet between, cockpit about 5½ feet, as shown. Dry stowage fore and aft, with hatches and mast tubes fore and aft, as shown. Hatches fasten at sides with metal straps and thumbscrews—with rubber tube ring packing between hatch and deck. No hatches over cockpit. Floor raised to be level with top of No. 1 Radix centerboard trunk. No air tanks, the dry stowage compartments serving instead. Air tanks and hatches for cockpit can be made for canoes built to order at an extra cost to purchaser of $7.00 for air tanks and $10.00 for hatches.

WREN MODEL.—Length, 16 feet; beam, 30 inches; depth at bow, 18½ inches; at center, 11 inches; at stern, 16 inches.

MODEL.—The aim of the builder of the WREN is to test the advantage, if any be found, in the shorter water line and marked curve of the keelson.

MATERIAL, CONSTRUCTION, FINISH, the same as VESPER, *except* bow stem steam bent oak and stern post from plank.

MEASUREMENTS—All lengths and beam, over all. All depths from base line at level with lowest part of keelson to top of gunwale.

CRUISING SAILING CANOE—WREN.

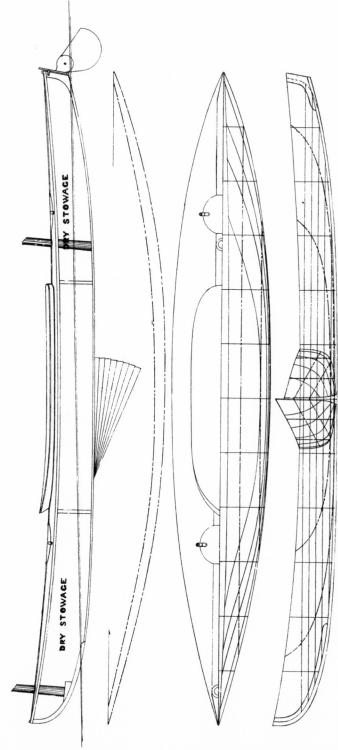

DRY STOWAGE

DRY STOWAGE

PRICE.—Including only mast tubes, plates and hatch fastenings, $100.00.
" No. 1 Radix centerboard, Drop Rudder No. 1, 4 cleats. Rigs No. 42 and 40 (single halliard), 106 sq ft., 9 foot double blade paddle with drip cups. Folding cushion of corduroy and hair, 30 inch sliding deck seat and steering gear No. 60, $164.00.

VESPER.

SAIL PLAN.

(Bailey improved sails, double halliard.)

CRUISING SAILING CANOES—VESPER.

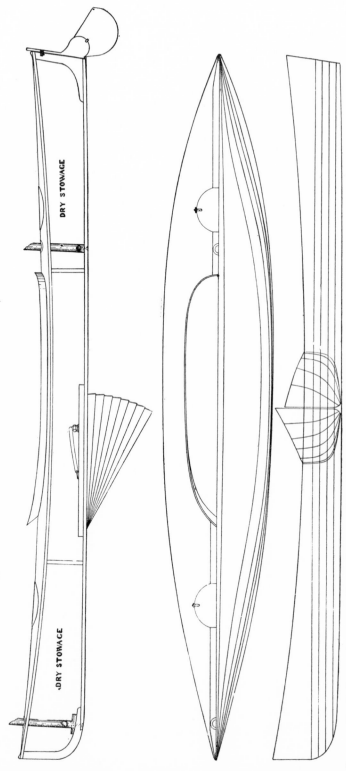

DRY STOWAGE

DRY STOWAGE

PRICE.—Including only mast tubes, plates and hatch fastenings, $100.00.
" No. 1 Radix centerboard, Drop Rudder No. 1 (not No. 3 as shown above), 4 cleats. Rigs No. 42 and 40 (double halliard), 106 sq. ft., 9 foot double blade paddle with drip cups. Folding cushion of corduroy, hair filled; 30 inch sliding deck seat, and steering gear No. 61, $170.00.

GENERAL DESCRIPTION OF SAILS, SPARS, ETC.

Sails—I am using the best brand (Langdon G. B.) bleached cotton for areas up to 100 square feet. Over that area bleached Wamsutta Drills. All sails bighted 10 inches unless otherwise required. Non-Elastic Web (instead of rope) is used on the edges of all sails, single on areas under 50 square feet, over that area on both sides.

Masts and Spars—Material: If 3 inches or upward in diameter, natural growth Spruce. Under that, best sawed Spruce. Sizes: Up to and including sail areas of 75 square feet to fit tubing of 2 inches inside diameter. Between 75 and 100 square feet, 2¼ inch; 100 and under 125 square feet, 2¾ inches, and 4 inches for areas of 125 feet and upward.

LATEEN RIGS.

While the Lateen is a handy and effective rig in small areas, on account of the length of spars required, it is not desirable in sizes over 50 square feet and is mostly used for mizzens, where only a few feet area is required to balance the mainsail. This sail will be rigged in two ways—call them A and B.

Style A—A very short mast with metal pin in top; a small ring lashed to the yard, about two-fifths the distance from connecting ring to peak, which hooks over the pin when sail is in position. A single (No. 24) jaw is attached to side of boom, a few inches aft of connecting ring, which engages the mast and holds the sail in position. The sheet rope completes the rig.

Style B—Has mast headgear (No. 11); foot gear (No. 12); boom fastener (No. 16), and hoists with a halliard.

Number.	Length on Boom.		Length on Yard.		Length on Leach.		Area Square Feet.	Price of Sail Only.	Price of Rig. Style A.	Price of Rig. Style B.
	Ft.	In.	Ft.	In.	Ft.	In.				
1	5	1½	5	5	6	0	13	$1 35	$4 25	$ 7 25
2	5	10½	6	6	6	10	17	1 75	4 75	7 75
3	6	9	7	8	7	10	23	2 20	5 50	8 50
4	7	7	8	6	9	0	30	2 65	6 25	9 25
5	8	3	9	3	9	6	35	3 00	7 00	10 00
6	9	3	10	6	11	0	45	3 75	7 75	10 75

GENERAL DESCRIPTION OF SAILS, CORDAGE, Etc.

CORDAGE.

FINE BRAIDED COTTON—"SAMPSON" MAKE.

No. 10,   about $\frac{3}{8}$ inch diameter, per yard ----- $0 05
" 9,   " $\frac{5}{16}$ "   " ----- 045
" 8,   " $\frac{9}{32}$ "   " ----- 04
" 7,   " $\frac{1}{4}$ "   " ----- 035
" 6,   " $\frac{7}{32}$ "   " ----- 03
" 5,   " $\frac{3}{16}$ "   " ----- 025
" 4,   " $\frac{5}{32}$ "   " ----- 02
" 3 ½,   " $\frac{1}{8}$ "   " ----- 015
" 0,   for lashing sails to spars,   " ----- 01

LEG O'MUTTON RIG.

The Leg o' Mutton or Mutton Leg rig is a very old one, and though not so much used as formerly, is still a favorite with many. The only objection to it being that it requires a very long mast for the area. This sail will be rigged in three ways—call them A, B and C.

STYLE A.—Just the sail lashed to the mast and a sheet rope fastened to the clew.
STYLE B.—Sail lashed to the mast and boom; boom connected to mast by boom fastener, (No. 17); sheet rope.
STYLE C.—Sheave in head of mast; mast rings; boom fastener (No. 17); sail hoists with halliard. Reef points if so ordered on style C.

Number.	Length on Boom.	Length on Mast.	Length on Leach.	Area Square Feet.	Price of Sail only.	Price of Rig Style A.	Price of Rig Style B	Price of Rig Style C.
7	4 Ft. 3 In.	7 Ft. 3 In.	7 Ft. 10 In.	15	$1 50	$3 25	$4 75	$6 75
8	5 Ft. 0 In.	8 Ft. 0 In.	8 Ft. 9 In.	20	2 00	4 00	5 50	7 50
9	5 Ft. 9 In.	8 Ft. 9 In.	9 Ft. 8 In.	25	2 50	4 75	6 25	8 25
10	6 Ft. 9 In.	10 Ft. 4 In.	12 Ft. 5 In.	35	3 00	5 50	7 25	9 50
11	8 Ft. 2 In.	12 Ft. 3 In.	13 Ft. 8 In.	50	4 00	6 50	8 25	10 75

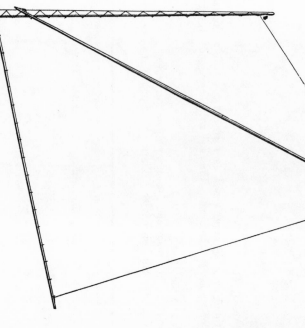

SPRIT SAIL RIG.

This is a very simple rig—cheap because it requires no metal fittings except boom fastener (No. 17) and mast clamps. It cannot be reefed. To lower the rig you go forward in the boat and remove the lower end of the sprit from the loop by which it is held to the mast; tip the boom up against the mast and lift the mast from the tube. It is a very effective rig and is used considerably on open skiffs, but not considered as safe as some others, because it cannot be lowered without shifting position in the boat.

Number.	Area.	Price, Sail Only.	Price Complete
12	15	$1 40	$4 75
13	25	2 25	5 50
14	40	3 50	6 25
15	50	4 25	7 00
16	65	5 50	8 00
17	80	6 50	9 25

FORE AND AFT OR GAFF RIG.

A common and well known rig for large areas. In suitable sizes, it is well adapted to small open boats and combination row and sail boats where but a single sail is wanted. It has no battens. Numbers 18, 19, 20 and 21 have each one row of reef points; numbers 22, 23 and 24 two each.

The boom fastener for this rig will be my No. 15, with block and plate (No. 44) to fasten to deck forward to carry the halliards. Mast rings are used and a clamp and block for throat and peak halliards. On Nos. 23 and 24 a block is put on the gaff, a double block at head of mast, and peak halliards are double from gaff to mast head. Wood jaws are used on gaff, as being lighter and better than metal.

Number.	Area.	Price Sail Only.	Price Complete.
18	40	$ 3 50	$12 00
19	50	4 25	13 00
20	60	5 00	14 00
21	75	6 00	17 00
22	100	8 00	20 00
23	125	10 00	25 00
24	150	12 00	27 00

55

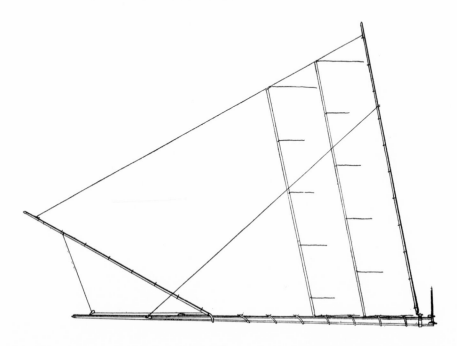

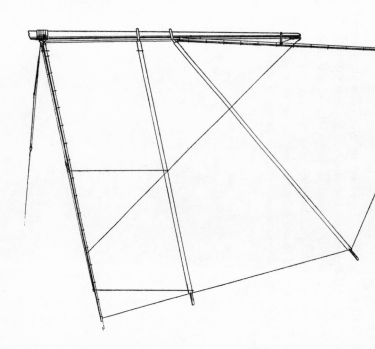

DESCRIPTION AND PRICES OF RIGS.

NEW CANOE SAIL.

Though no longer new, has always been a popular rig because of its short spars and perfect working, whether whole or reefed. It sets very flat and is very effective. Head Gear No. 11, Foot Gear No. 12, Boom Fastener No. 17 and Mast Clamps are used on this rig.

Number.	Area.	Price, sail only	Price complete
25	20	$2 00	$11 00
26	25	2 50	11 50
27	45	3 75	13 50
28	60	5 00	15 00
29	75	6 50	16 50

REEFING GEAR—It is contemplated to use a reefing gear on rigs 25 to 44 inclusive, and such blocks, sheaves, cordage, &c., as are required for that purpose are covered by the prices named for these rigs, but such fittings as cleats, &c., that attach to the boat, are extra.

DESCRIPTION AND PRICES OF RIGS.

THE BAILEY RIG, DOUBLE HALLIARDS.

We have so called it because we first made it to drawings furnished by Mr. Reade W. Bailey. It is a decidedly popular rig among racers. By using our double head and spar gear, with double halliards, we bring the yard perpendicular and against the mast. The sail sets very smoothly, and the center of effort being low down, it is very effective. Numbers 38 and 39 have two battens. Reef lines at lower batten unless otherwise ordered.

Spar Gear No. 13, Head Gear No. 14, Foot Gear No. 15 with a double block on plate attached to the deck forward of the mast are used on this rig.

Number.	Area.	Price, sail only.	Price complete.
35	30	$3 00	$13 00
36	40	3 75	14 00
37	60	5 00	16 00
38	75	6 50	17 50
39	90	7 50	19 00

57

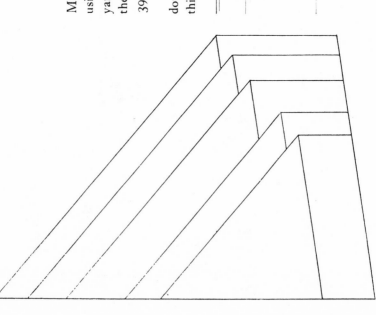

DESCRIPTION AND PRICES OF RIGS.

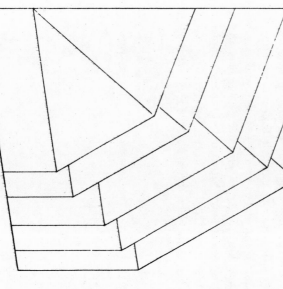

IMPROVED BAILEY RIG, DOUBLE HALLIARDS.

See also cut of Vesper, page 50.

This is like the Bailey rigs Nos. 35–39, EXCEPT in the shape of the leach between batten and peak, and the use of another batten as shown. This change of shape increases the area on the same length of spars. It is, without doubt, the most effective and popular sail in use at the present date.

Number.	Area.	Price, sail only.	Price complete.
40	36	$3 50	$14 00
41	47	4 25	15 00
42	70	5 75	17 50
43	87	7 50	20 00
44	103	9 00	22 00

Fitted and rigged the same as Nos. 35–39.

DESCRIPTION AND PRICES OF RIGS.

To bring the yard close to and parallel with the mast, double halliards are required, but as some prefer the single halliard I will duplicate Rigs Nos. 35 to 44 inclusive, with single halliard, cutting the sail on the yard at a slight angle as required.

The method of rigging will be with a sheave in mast head and single block on the deck forward of the mast. The halliard, fastening to the yard, will lead over the sheave in mast head, thence down and through block on deck, thence forward or aft as required for main or mizzen, to hand or cleat.

The same mast footgear and the same reef gear will be used as on Nos. 35–44, but mast head gear No. 14 and spar gear No. 13 will be dispensed with, thereby lessening the cost a little. Each will be known by the same number as its corresponding area with double halliard, but with the letter "B" annexed—as No. 35 for 30-foot sail with double halliard and No. 35 B for 30-foot with single halliard.

THE BAILEY RIG, SINGLE HALLIARD.

Number.	Area.	Price, sail only.	Price complete.
35 B	30	$3 00	$11 00
36 B	40	3 75	12 00
37 B	60	5 00	14 00
38 B	75	6 50	15 00
39 B	90	7 50	17 00

IMPROVED BAILEY RIG, SINGLE HALLIARD.

Number.	Area.	Price, sail only.	Price complete.
40 B	36	$3 50	$12 00
41 B	47	4 25	13 00
42 B	70	5 75	15 50
43 B	87	7 50	18 00
44 B	103	9 00	20 00

59

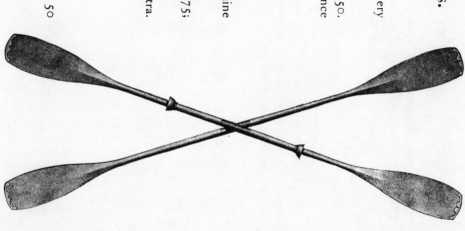

PADDLES—Description and Prices.

SINGLE BLADE PADDLES.

Hand-made from choice maple, oiled and varnished. Very fine.

Length, 4½, 4¾, 5, 5¼, 5½ feet. Price, each, $1.50. Other lengths or special patterns made to order at proper advance for special work.

DOUBLE BLADE PADDLES.

Made from clear spruce, friction joint, copper machine locked tips, oiled and varnished, without drip cups.

7, 7½, 8 feet, each, $3.25; 8½ feet, $3.50; 9 feet, $3.75; 9½ feet, $4.00; 10 feet, $4.50.

Square point double blades made *to order* 25 cents extra. Spoon blades, square pointed, 75 cents extra.

RUBBER DRIP CUPS—As Shown.

For double blade paddles, per pair,   -   -   -   - $0 50

OARS—DESCRIPTION AND PRICES.

SPRUCE OARS, SPOON BLADE. (Fig. 1.)

6, 6½, 7 feet, copper tipped and varnished, per pair -	$3 50
7½ " " " " " -	3 75
8 " " " " " -	4 00
8½ " " " " " -	4 25
9 " " " " " -	4 50
9½ " " " " " -	4 75
Leathered, per pair *extra*, - - -	50

The spoon oars are *hand-made* from the very best of stock, and finely finished, oiled varnished and copper tipped.

SPRUCE OARS, STRAIGHT BLADE. (Fig. 2.)

6, 6½ and 7 feet, copper tipped and varnished, per pair,	$2 00
7½ and 8 " " " "	2 25
8½ and 9 " " " "	2 50
Leathered, *extra*, - - - -	50

SPRUCE OARS, STRAIGHT BLADE, SQUARE LOOM. (Fig. 3.)

6, 6½ and 7 feet, copper tipped and varnished, per pair,	$2 50
7½ and 8 " " " "	2 75
8½ and 9 " " " "	3 00

MAPLE OARS, STRAIGHT BLADE, SQUARE LOOM. (Fig. 4.)

7½ feet, varnished, per pair, - -	$3 25
8 " " " - -	3 50
8½ " " " - -	3 75
9 " " " - -	4 00

61

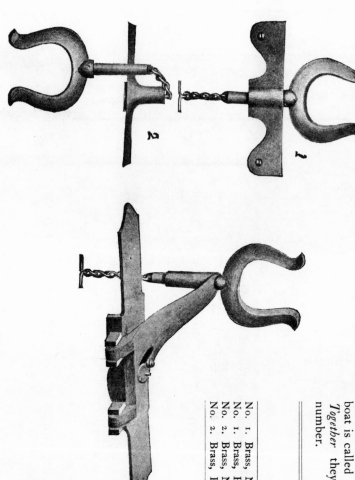

ROWLOCKS.—Description and Prices.

Definitions.—That part which is fastened to the boat is called the Socket. The other part the Oarlock. *Together* they are termed Rowlocks. Please order by number.

	Oarlocks Only.	Sockets Only.	Rowlocks Complete.
No. 1. Brass, Nickel-plated, per pr.	$1 25	$1 25	$2 50
No. 1. Brass, Polished, "	1 15	1 15	2 25
No. 2. Brass, Nickel-plated, "	1 25	1 40	2 50
No. 2. Brass, Polished, "	1 15	1 25	2 25

OUTRIGGERS.

These Outriggers have a spread of 8 inches per pair, outside the gunwales. When not in use, they may be turned down inside the boat. (Screw holes in plate not shown.)

Price per pair, Polished Brass, - - - $5 50
" " " Nickel-plated Brass, - - - 6 00

All sockets are drilled for 9-16 in. pin. If ordering to replace worn-out or broken parts, remember this.

ROWLOCKS—DESCRIPTION AND PRICES.

	Oarlocks Only.	Sockets Only.	Rowlocks Complete
No. 3. Brass, Nickel-plated, per pair -----	$1 50	$1 25	$2 75
No. 3. " Polished, " -----	1 40	1 15	2 50
No. 4. " Nickel-plated, " -----	1 50	1 25	2 75
No. 4. " Polished, " -----	1 40	1 15	2 50
No. 5. " Nickel-plated, " -----	1 25	1 25	2 50
No. 5. " Polished, " -----	1 15	1 15	2 25

Rowlock No. 5 is intended for Dinghys. It is nearly like No. 1 in pattern, but the socket goes on the inwale and does not project outside the gunwale.

OARLOCKS Nos. 3 and 4 have a spread of 1½, 1¾ and 2 inches. In ordering state which is wanted.

All sockets are drilled for 9-16 in. pin. If ordering to replace worn-out or broken parts, remember this.

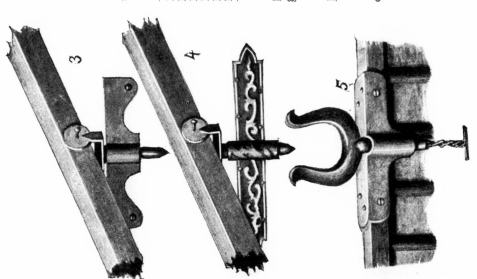

63

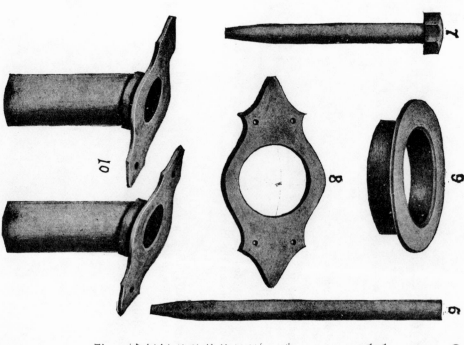

CANOE FITTINGS—DESCRIPTION AND PRICES.

MAST PINS.

	PRICE.
With Nut (Fig. 7) - - - - - - -	$0 30
Without Nut (Fig. 6) - - - - - -	0 25

MAST PLATES.

Inside Diameter.		Fig. 9.	No. 8.
1 ½ inches	- -	$0 30	$0 35
1 ¾ "	- -	30	35
2 · "	- -	30	35
2 ¼ "	- -	40	50
2 ½ "	- -	50	60
2 ¾ "	- -	60	75
3 "	- -	70	90
3 ½ "	- -	80	1 05
4 "	- -	90	1 20

FLAG TUBES AND PLATES (Fig. 10)—Tube 3 inches deep, 1 inch inside diameter. Price 75 cents each.

(Screw holes not shown in Fig. 9.)

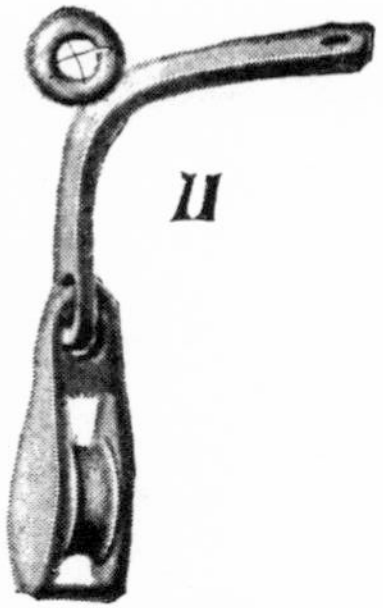

CANOE FITTINGS—DESCRIPTION AND PRICES.

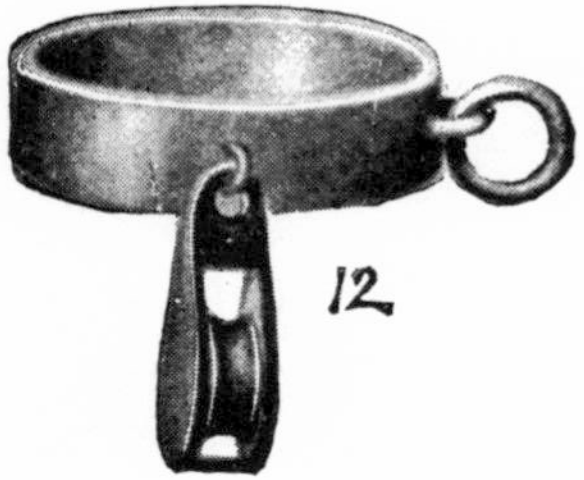

MAST AND SPAR GEAR.

(Patented.)

Mast Head Gear (Fig. 11) Double Block	- - -	$0 75
" " " Double Block	- - -	1 00
(Fig. 14) Band 1⅜ inch	- - -	2 00
Mast Foot Gear, 1¾, 2, 2¼ inch (Fig. 12)	- - -	$0 75
" " " " Double Block	-	1 00
Mast Foot Gear (Fig. 15), 2 inch	-	$2 25
" 2¼ "	-	2 25
" 2½ "	-	2 50
" 2¾ "	-	2 75
" 3 "	-	3 00
" 3¼ "	-	3 00
" 3½ "	-	3 25
" 4 "	-	3 50

Sizes above three inches have no reef block.

Gaff or Spar Gear (Fig 13), sizes to fit spar 1, 1⅛, 1¼, 1⅜, and 1½ inches diameter, each $2.25.

NOTE—The screw attachment, as shown, between the parts, has been changed. A nut and check-nut underneath the arm is now used.

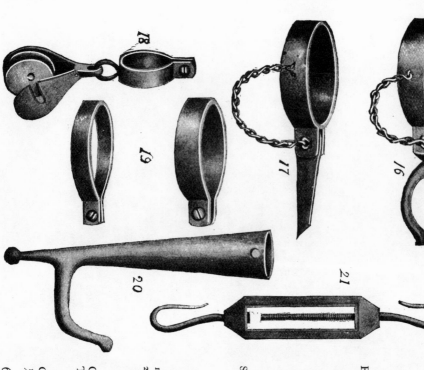

CANOE FITTINGS—DESCRIPTION AND PRICES.

BOOM FASTENING.

(Patented.)

Boom fastening and clamp (Fig. 16),	1 ¾	and 2 inch			$ 75
" " " "	" 2½	and 3 inch			90
" " " "	" 3½	inch			1 00
" " " "	" 4	inch			1 25
" " " spike (Fig. 17),	1 ¾	and 2 inch			60
" " " "	" 2½	and 3 inch			75
" " " "	" 3½	inch			1 00
" " " "	" 4	inch			1 25

SPAR GEAR.

Spar gear (Fig. 18),	¾ to 1¼ clamp	$1 00
" " "	1⅜ to 1¾ clamp	1 15

MAST CLAMPS.

(Fig. 19.)

To be used for holding foot gear and boom fastenings in place.

1 ¾, 2 and 2¼ inch, per set of 3 pieces	$ 75
2½ inch	90

Larger sizes to order at increased price.

BOAT HOOKS.

Canoe size (Fig. 20)	$1 00
The same complete with 8-foot pole	1 50

TURNBUCKLES.

Canoe size (Fig. 21), per pair	$1 00
¼ inch, per pair	1 50

CANOE FITTINGS—DESCRIPTION AND PRICES.

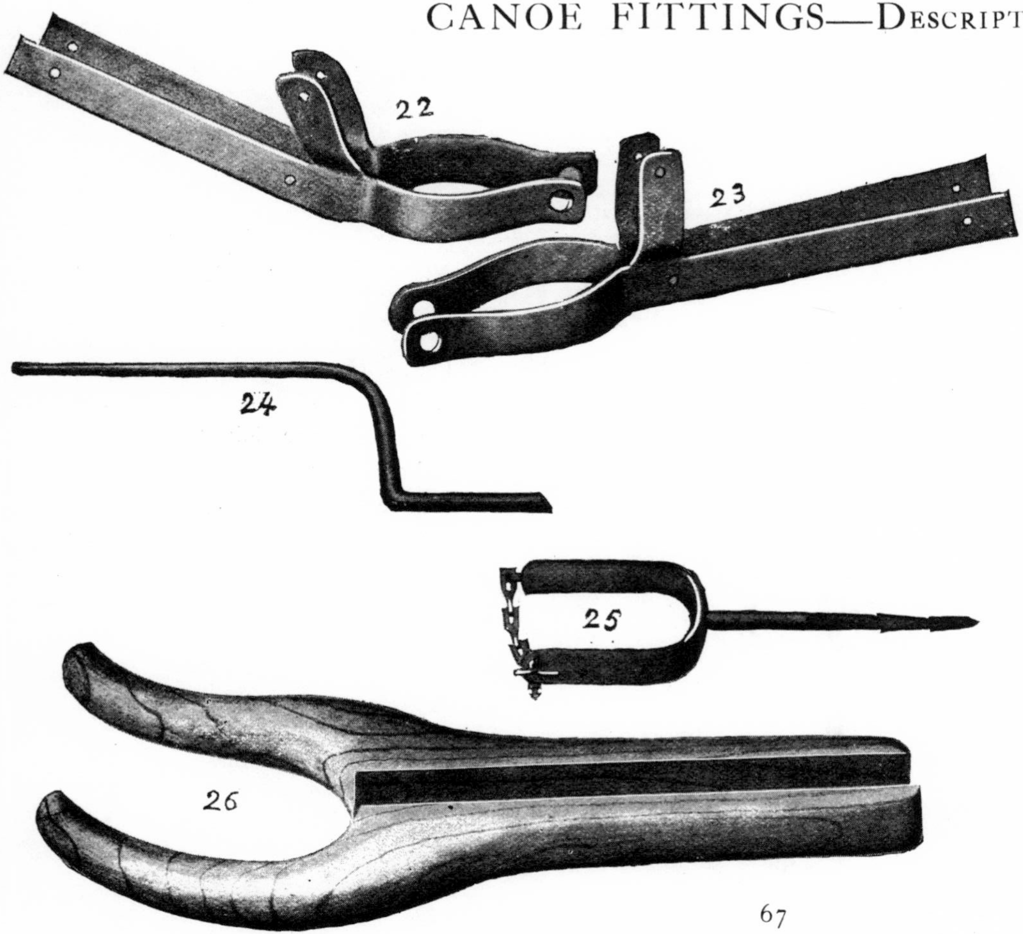

JAWS.

Bailey (Figs. 22–23), 2 pieces for 1 ¾ and 2 in.
mast --$1 00
Bailey (Figs. 22–23), 2 pieces for 2 ¼ in. mast.. 1 10
Bailey (Figs. 22–23), 2 pieces for 2 ½ in. mast.. 1 25
Bailey (Figs. 22–23), 2 pieces for 3 in. mast.. 1 40
Bailey (Figs. 22–23), 2 pieces for 3 ½ in. mast.. 1 50
Fig. 22 for New Canoe Sail.

Single (Fig. 24), for 1 ¾ inch mast --------$0 30
   "   "   "   2   "   "   -------------- .35
   "   "   "   2 ½ "   "   -------------- .50

Double (Fig. 25), 1 ½, 1 ¾ and 2 inch --------$0 50
   "   "   2 ¼, 2 ½   "   -------------- 60
   "   "   "   3   "   -------------- 80
   "   "   "   3 ½   "   -------------- 90
   "   "   "   4   "   -------------- 1 50

For Gaff Rig, wood, 2 ¾ inch mast --------$1 00
   "   "   "   "   4   "   "   -------------- 1 50

FIG. 26.

67

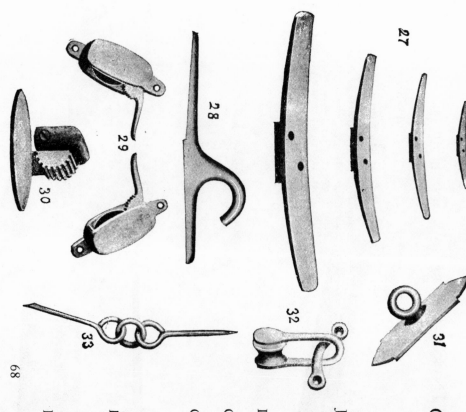

CANOE FITTINGS--DESCRIPTION AND PRICES.

CLEATS.

						PRICE.
Jam Cleats (Fig. 27), 2 inches	-	-	-	-	-	$0 12
" " " 3 "	-	-	-	-	-	18
" " " 4 "	-	-	-	-	-	25
" " " 5 "	-	-	-	-	-	30
" " " 6 "	-	-	-	-	-	35
Improved "Butler" Cleats (Fig. 28), about 3 inches long	-	-	-	-	-	30
Clutch Cleats (Fig. 29), right and left hand, screw on side of coaming, each	-	-	-	-	-	60
Clam Cleats (Fig. 30), Canoe size	-	-	-	-	-	40
" " " Cruiser size	-	-	-	-	-	50

DANDY FAIRLEADERS.

Figs. 31 and 32 (order by these numbers), each $0 30

CONNECTING RINGS.

For yard and booms (Fig. 33)   -   - $0 25

CANOE FITTINGS—Description and Prices.

BLOCKS.

	PRICE.
Reef, single (Fig. 34)	$0 20
" double (Fig. 35)	30
¼ inch blocks (Fig. 36)	30
⅜ " " (Fig. 36)	35
½ " " (Fig. 36)	50
¼ " double blocks (Fig. 37)	40
⅜ " " " (Fig. 37)	45
½ " " " (Fig. 37)	70
¼ or ⅜ in. swivel blocks (Fig. 38)	45
Cam blocks (Fig. 39)	50
No. 1, snatch block for ¼ or ⅜	
inch cord (Fig. 40)	35
No. 2, snatch block for ¼ or ⅜	
inch cord (Fig. 41)	50
Double snatch block for ¼ or ⅜	
inch cord (Fig. 42)	90

BLOCKS ON PLATE.

	PRICE.
Single (Fig. 43)	$0 80
Double (Fig. 44)	1 00

Larger sizes, swivel or special patterns, to order.

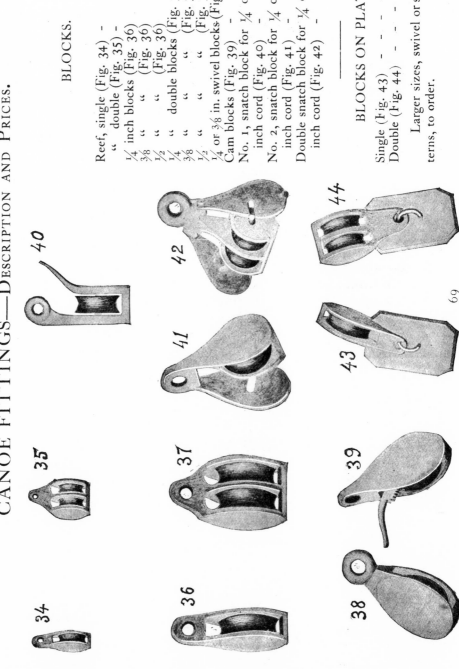

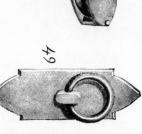

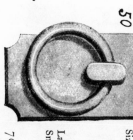

CANOE FITTINGS—DESCRIPTION

AND PRICES.

SWIVEL SHEET BLOCK WITH CLAMP FOR BOOM.

	PRICE.
Small Size (Fig. 45), ¼ inch cord - - -	$1 10
Large " " ⅜ " " - - -	1 25

SWIVEL SHEET BLOCK ON PLATE.

Small Size (Fig. 46), ¼ inch cord - - -	$0 85
Large " " ⅜ " " - - -	1 00

CHOCKS.

Canoe size (Fig. 47), about 3 inch	STRAIGHT OR BEVELED.	- - -	$0 40
Size, about 4½ inch (Fig 48)	STRAIGHT OR BEVELED.	- - -	$0 60

SHEET RINGS.

Large sheet rings (Fig. 50) - - -	$0 45
Small sheet rings (Fig. 49) - - -	35

Screw holes not shown in Nos. 48, 49, 50.

CAST BRASS, POLISHED AND NICKEL-PLATED FIGURES AND LETTERS. (Fig. 51.)

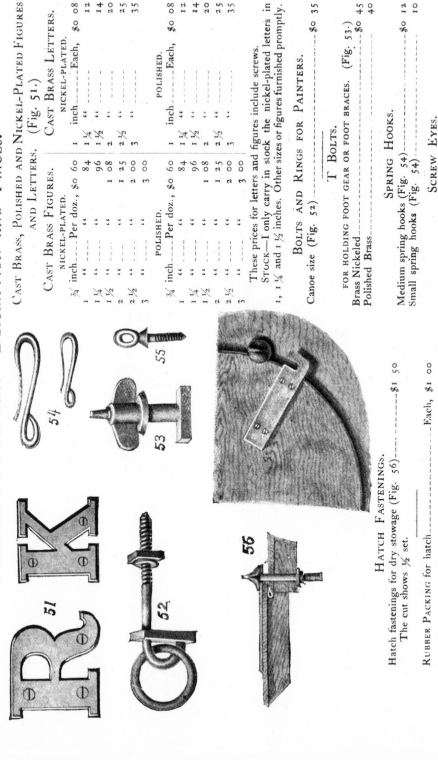

CAST BRASS FIGURES.

NICKEL-PLATED.

3/4 inch — Per doz.,	$0 60
1 "	84
1 1/4 "	96
1 1/2 "	1 08
2 "	1 25
2 1/2 "	2 00
3 "	3 00

POLISHED.

3/4 inch — Per doz.,	$0 60
1 "	84
1 1/4 "	96
1 1/2 "	1 08
2 "	1 25
2 1/2 "	2 00
3 "	3 00

CAST BRASS LETTERS.

NICKEL-PLATED.

1 inch — Each,	$0 08
1 1/4 "	12
1 1/2 "	14
2 "	20
2 1/2 "	25
3 "	35

POLISHED.

1 inch — Each,	$0 08
1 1/4 "	12
1 1/2 "	14
2 "	20
2 1/2 "	25
3 "	35

These prices for letters and figures include screws.

STOCK—I only carry in stock the nickel-plated letters in 1, 1 1/4 and 1 1/2 inches. Other sizes or figures furnished promptly.

BOLTS AND RINGS FOR PAINTERS.

Canoe size (Fig. 52) - - - - - - $0 35

T BOLTS.

FOR HOLDING FOOT GEAR OR FOOT BRACES. (Fig. 53.)

Brass Nickeled - - - - - - $0 45
Polished Brass - - - - - - 40

SPRING HOOKS.

Medium spring hooks (Fig. 54) - - - - - $0 12
Small spring hooks (Fig. 54) - - - - - 10

SCREW EYES.

Screw Eyes (Fig. 55) - - - - - - $0 68

HATCH FASTENINGS.

Hatch fastenings for dry stowage (Fig. 56) - - - - - $1 50
The cut shows 1/2 set.
RUBBER PACKING for hatch - - - - - Each, $1 00

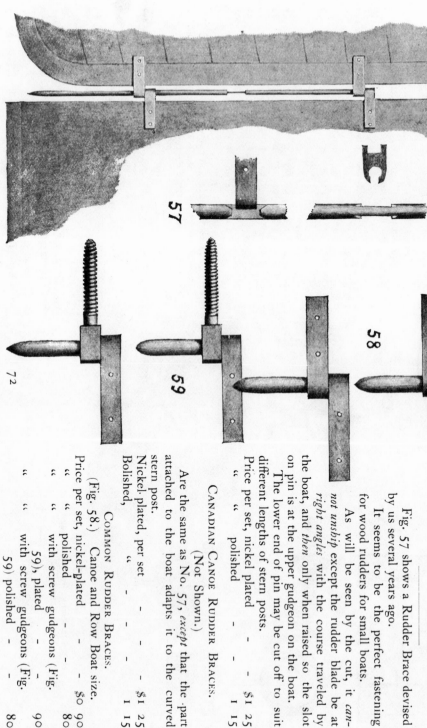

57

58

59

RUDDER BRACES.

DESCRIPTION AND PRICES.

Fig. 57 shows a Rudder Brace devised by us several years ago.

It seems to be the perfect fastening for wood rudders for small boats.

As will be seen by the cut, it can-*not unship* except the rudder blade be at *right angles* with the course traveled by the boat, and *then* only when raised so the slot on pin is at the upper gudgeon on the boat.

The lower end of pin may be cut off to suit different lengths of stern posts.

Price per set, nickel plated - - - $1 25
    "   "   polished - - -   1 15

CANADIAN CANOE RUDDER BRACES.
(Not Shown.)

Are the same as No. 57, *except* that the part attached to the boat adapts it to the curved stern post.

Nickel-plated, per set - - - - $1 25
Bolished,   "   "   - - -   1 15

COMMON RUDDER BRACES.

(Fig. 58.) Canoe and Row Boat size.
Price per set, nickel-plated - - $0 90
    "   "   polished - - -   80
    "   "   with screw gudgeons (Fig. 59), plated - - -   90
    "   "   with screw gudgeons (Fig. 59) polished - - -   80

METAL AND WOOD RUDDERS—Description and Prices.

DROP RUDDERS.

Canoe size, No. 1 - - - - - $7 00
Row boat size, No. 2 - - - - - 8 50

This is the best and strongest drop rudder in the market.

WOOD RUDDERS.

Size for row boats and canoes, including braces and cross heads.

Cherry or Maple, with No. 57 braces - - $2 50
Cherry or Maple, with Nos. 58 or 59 braces - - 2 00
Spruce, natural crook, according to size, and braces $2 50 to 5 00

1 & 2

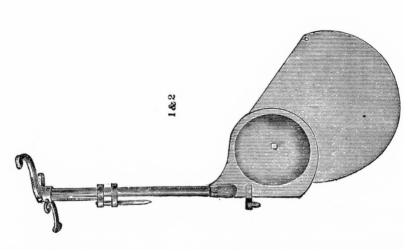

DECK STEERING GEAR—DESCRIPTION AND PRICES.

DECK STEERING GEAR. No. 60.

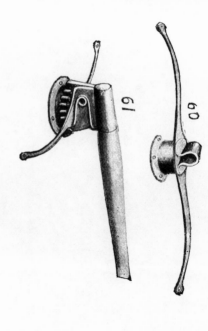

Fitted with oak or maple stick.

	PRICE.
Gear and handle only - - - -	$2 50
Including Safety Chain, Hooks and Tighteners - - -	4 25

SELF-LOCKING DECK STEERING GEAR, No. 61.

PATENTED.

Gear and Handle only - - - - -	$4 00
Including Safety Chain, Hooks and Tighteners - -	6 00

The spring locks it, and the natural pressure of the hand upon the end of the tiller releases it, when it can be turned as freely as the other gear.

FOLDING CENTERBOARD.

RADIX PATENT FOLDING CENTERBOARD.

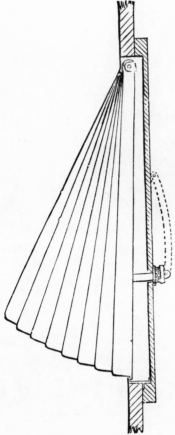

Size	Weight	Area	Width of slot	Price
15 x 30 in.	9 lbs.	1 ⅝ Sq. Ft.	1⁵⁄₁₆ req'd in keel	12.00
18 x 36 in.	12 "	2 ¼ " "	1⅛ " "	15.00
24 x 37 in.	15 "	4 " "	1 ¼ " "	20.00

74

Thwartship Deck Steering Gear.—Description and Prices.

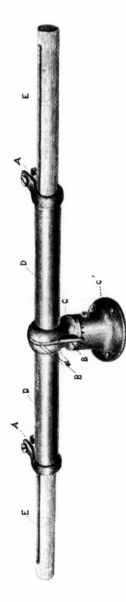

(Invented by J. H. Rushton, 1901.)

The base, "C'," screws firmly to the deck at any convenient point aft the cockpit. Its hollow center engages the lower part of "C," and allows it to turn freely. To "C" on either side are brazed the lengths of tube "DD" through which the stick "E" passes and turns freely. The locking device or pawl, "B," is a separate piece and by taking out the stick "E" can be removed entirely. A slot in one side of the stick "E" (lined with metal) engages a projection on the pawl "B," and a slight turn of the stick locks or unlocks the gear.

To Make It Self Locking.—Slip a stiff rubber band over "B" and "C." Then you can slip the band down and off from both, if you do not want a *self* locking gear, or up over "C" but *under* "B" if you would prevent locking. This is three kinds of gear in one, and the changes made without cost, anywhere, in a moment's time. Connections with gear and rudder yoke may be made with cord, chain, or a solid stick on one side only.

Price, Gear only, $5.00.

75

BOAT SEAT CUSHIONS.

MATERIAL.—Gray Corduroy, filled with best curled hair or cork shavings. Prices, according to size and shape—$2.50 to $4.00 each. Other material also may be used, and prices vary accordingly, ranging from $1.00 to $10.00 each.

FOLDING CUSHIONS.

Size (each part) 12 x 15 inches; material, gray corduroy, hair filled, $4.00··

FOLDING SEATS.

Cherry frame, cane bottom and back	-	-	-	$4 00
Cherry	-	-	-	2 50
Ash, or other suitable wood	-	-	-	1 50

Bottom and back may be made solid, as shown, or of strips about two inches wide and separated a little (at option of maker).

BOAT COVER.—This is made of No. 10 canvas, unpainted. The top is shaped to the boat and to the sides to follow sheer line. It is then seamed at gunwales and at ends. If the boat rests on the floor the lower edge of the cover reach nearly to it. It is made somewhat larger than the boat because of probable shrinkage subsequently.

PRICE.—For boat under 44 inch beam per foot of length - - - $0 40
For boat 44 to 50 inch beam per foot of length - - - 50
For boat 51 to 60 inch beam per foot of length - - - 60

SEATS, SEAT BACKS, FOOT BRACES.

CANE SEATS AND EASY BACKS.

The frame is made of cherry, oak or ash, according to grade of boat, or as may be ordered.

Boat seat only, according to size	$1.25 to 1.50
Back only, without straps or hinges	1.25
Back with straps and hinges	2.25
Back for stern seat, small	1.00

SLIDING DECK SEAT.

30 inch, for sailing canoes	$5 00

FOOT BRACES.

Including brass T bolt	$0 50

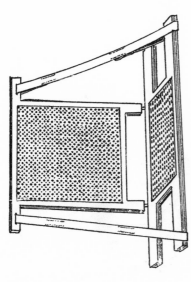

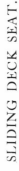

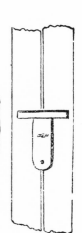

77

SUNDRY FITTINGS—Description and Prices.

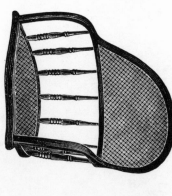

CHAIR SEATS.

Chair Seat No. 1, cane bottom and back, each -	$3 00
Chair Seat No. 2, cane bottom, spindle back, each -	2 00

AWNING. CARPET. CANVAS.

Awning Tubes and plates - - -	$4 00
Awning, with sticks and posts - $7 50 to 12 00
Carpet, Body Brussels - - -	5 00 to 10 00
Canvas, (painted), used instead of carpet,	5 00 to 8 00

CARRYING YOKES.

MADE FROM SOLID BLOCK.

Basswood, *used with Hunting Canoe or Saranac Laker*, $2 50

SAFETY CHAIN.

Brass Safety Chain, No. 1, nickel-plated, per foot - $0 10

SEAT BRACES.

Brass, fancy pattern, nickel-plated, each - -	$0 30
Brass, nickeled, each - - - -	20
Polished, each - - - - -	16
Galvanized Iron, each - - - -	10

SUNDRY FITTINGS—Description and Prices.

AIR TANKS.

These are made of thin sheet copper placed over a box of thin wood to give proper shape. *They must be fitted to the boat.*

For Canoes under 31 inch beam, per pair - - $ 8 00

" Boats 32 to 36	" " "	- -	8 50
" " 37 to 42	" " "	- -	9 00
" " 43 to 48	" " "	- -	10 00
" " 49 to 54	" " "	- -	12 00
" " 55 to 60	" " "	- -	15 00

For Square Stern Boats add 25 per cent. to above prices.

STEM BANDS OR BANG IRONS.

Cut from sheet brass; about an inch wide at keel, tapering to about ⅜ inch at deck; thickness about No. 11, B. & S.

Nickeled, 30, 38 and 42 inches, each - - $1 00
Polished, 30, 38 and 42 " " - - 90
* " 19 " " - - 45

Special sizes or patterns extra.

*The lower half of Bang Iron; to reach above water line.

METAL RAILING.

Nickel-plated brass, per set - - - - $

A SET consists of 16 stanchions about 3 inches high and 4 pieces of tubing, each ⅜x48 inches, with ornamental button at each end of tubing.

RINGS—SOLID BRASS NICKEL PLATED.

½ and ¾ inch inside diameter, each - - -	$0	06
1 and 1¼ " " " " - - -		08
1½ " " " " - - -		10
1¾ " " " " - - -		12
2 and 2¼ " " " " - - -		15
2½ " " " " - - -		20
2¾ and 3 " " " " - - -		25
3½ and 4 " " " " - - -		30
4½ " " " " - - -		35

FERRULES.

⅜, ½, ⅝, ¾ and ⅞ inch, each - - -	$0	05
1, 1⅛, 1¼, 1⅜ and 1½ inch, each - - -		10
1¾ to 2½ inch, each - - -		15

FRICTION JOINTS.

Joints, for spars and masts. Outside diameter given. All 6 inches long except 2, 2¼ and 2½ inches—those are 8 inches.

¾, ⅞, 1⅛ and 1$\frac{3}{16}$ inches - - -	$0	25
1¼ and 1$\frac{5}{16}$ inches - - -		40
1⅜ and 1$\frac{7}{16}$ inches - - -		50
1½ inches " " - - -		60
2 " " - - -		60
2¼ " " - - -		60

79

INDEX.

PAGE.

Selection, use and care of a boat --- 4
Pleasure Boats, Models, Etc., --- 5
Pleasure Boats; Grades--- 6-7
Combination Row and Sail Boats
Livery Rowboat--- 23-25
Saranac Laker --- 8-9-10
Idaho, Rowboat--- 11
Idaho, Combination --- 12-13
Florida, Rowboat --- 26
Florida, Combination --- 14-15
Iowa, Rowboat --- 16-17
Iowa Combination --- 27
Dinghy, Square Stern Boat, 18-19-27
Islander --- 20
Cat Boat --- 21-22
Paddling Canoes, Decking, Etc --- 28
War Canoe --- 29
Huron --- 38
St. Regis, Bucktail --- 39-40
Nessmuk, Indian --- 41-42
Vaux, Vaux, Jr.--- 37
Ontario --- 30-31
Arkansaw Traveler --- 36
Igo --- 32-33
Ugo--- 34-35
Indian --- 43
Canvas Covered--- 43-47
Sailing Canoes --- 48
Vesper --- 50-51
Wren --- 49

BOAT AND CANOE FITTINGS.

PAGE.

Rigs—Bailey --- 57-59
Bailey Improved --- 58-59
Gaff, or Fore and Aft --- 55
Lateen, Leg o'Mutton --- 52-53
New Canoe --- 56
Sprit --- 54
Mast, Spars, &c. --- 52

A
Adirondack Rowlocks --- 63
Air Tanks --- 79
Awning --- 78

B
Bang Irons or Stem Bands --- 79
Blocks --- 20
Boat Hooks --- 66
Boom Fastenings --- 66
Boat Cover --- 76

C
Cane Seats and Backs --- 77
Canvas for Inside Floor --- 78
Carpets --- 78
Carrying Yokes --- 78
Centerboard, Radix --- 74
Chair Seats --- 78
Chocks --- 70
Cleats --- 68
Connecting Rings --- 68
Cordage --- 53
Cushions --- 76

PAGE.

D
Deck Steering Gear --- 74-75
Drip Cups—Rubber --- 60

F
Fairleaders --- 68
Ferrules --- 79
Figures, Metal --- 71
Flag Staff Tubes and Plates --- 64
Folding Seats --- 76
Foot Braces --- 77

H
Hatch Fastenings --- 71
Hooks, Spring --- 71

J
Jaws --- 69
Joints --- 66

L
Letters --- 71

M
Mast Clamps --- 78
Mast Gear --- 78
Mast Pins --- 74
Mast Plates --- 78

O
Oars --- 68
Oarlocks --- 62-63
Outriggers --- 76

PAGE.

P
Paddles, single blade --- 60
Paddles, double blade --- 60

R
Railing, Brass, Nickel-plated --- 79
Rings --- 79
Ringbolts --- 71
Rowlocks --- 62-63
Rudders --- 73
Rudder Braces --- 72
Rudder Yokes --- 78

S
Safety Chain --- 78
Screw Eyes --- 71
Seat Braces --- 78
Sheet Rings --- 67
Sliding Deck Seat --- 79
Spar Gear --- 77
Swivel Sheet Block and Clamp --- 65-66
Swivel Sheet Block and Plate --- 70

T
T Bolts --- 71
Turnbuckles --- 56